# BERLITZ®

# KENYA

D0048420

- A  in the text denotes a highly recommended sight
- A complete A–Z of practical information starts on p.115
- Extensive mapping throughout: on cover flaps and in text

Berlitz Trademark Reg. US Patent Office and in other countries – Marca Registrada.
Printed in Switzerland by Weber SA, Bienne.

1st edition (1994/95)

**Although we make every effort to ensure the accuracy of the information in this guide, changes do occur. If you have any new information, suggestions or corrections to contribute, we would like to hear from you. Please write to Berlitz Publishing at the above address.**

| | |
|---|---|
| Text: | Donna Dailey |
| Editor: | Delphine Verroest |
| Photography: | Lawrence Lawry, except those on pp. 7, 45 (top), 53, 102, 103 and 105 by Donna Dailey, and pp. 12 and 86 © Berlitz |
| Cartography: | Falk-Verlag, Hamburg |
| Inside cover illustrations: | Oxford Illustrators |
| Layout: | Cristina Silva |

| | |
|---|---|
| Thanks to: | Kenya Airways, Kenya Wildlife Service, African Tours & Hotels Ltd, Lonrho Hotels Kenya Ltd, African Safari Trails, Kenya National Tourist Office and Jack Altman for their assistance and contribution in the preparation of this guide. |

| | |
|---|---|
| Cover photograph: | Flamingos on Lake Bogoria (Rift Valley) © Tony Stone Photolibrary – London |

# CONTENTS

# Kenya and the Kenyans

Travel through Kenya, and you will see all of Africa in one country. Roughly two and a half times the size of Great Britain, this East African republic is a cornucopia of landscapes and cultures strung like brightly coloured Maasai beads between the sun-baked Swahili coast and the shores of Lake Victoria. If you drive cross country, you will be surprised at how quickly the landscape changes: dropping down suddenly from fertile highlands into semi-arid plains, emerging from a lush mountain forest to sweep through a vast plateau, climbing up a steep escarpment from the deep, wide trench of the Rift Valley, or turning off tarmac lined with coconut palms on to a dusty, red-dirt road.

Kenya is a country of contradictions, where snow lies on the equator and semi-deserts flood in the long rains. Blue lakes turn suddenly pink when blanketed with a million flamingos; the icy top of Mount Kilimanjaro shimmers over Amboseli's parched plains. In contrast to the rich diversity of the south-west – home to 85 percent of the population – the vast northern and eastern regions, nearly two-thirds of the country, are arid wilderness.

The country has long been a favourite safari destination. Big game hunting expeditions are a thing of the past, and the only shooting allowed today is with a camera. But even with the rigours of the bush eased by organized game runs and reasonably comfortable safari vans, not much can match the thrill of seeing your first herd of elephants or pride of lions in the wild.

If, on the other hand, you want nothing more demanding from your holiday than to lie under a palm tree and run your toes through clean, white sand, Kenya's coastline offers long stretches of unspoiled beach and fantastic coral reefs, interspersed with comfortable resorts that cater to your every hedonistic desire.

**5**

Kenya's equatorial climate ranges from the saturating torpor of Mombasa to the heady, bracing air of the cool highlands around Nairobi. Although the capital is less than 150km (90 miles) from the equator, at over a mile above sea level you will most probably need a jacket in the evenings.

With more than 40 tribes and tribal languages, Kenya's national heritage is a patchwork quilt of history and customs, sewn together by the

*K*enyan contrasts: the red, dusty roads of Tsavo National Park and (right) a fruit seller on **6** Mombasa Beach.

colonial threads of the late 19th and early 20th centuries. Tribal differences are Kenya's greatest cultural asset, and one of its most formidable social and political challenges. Surprisingly, perhaps, the tribes are formations that rarely go back more than a couple of hundred years and were sustained as elements of colonial administration at a time when they were progressively merging and dissolving.

The divisions that Kenyans themselves make in defining their origins are mainly linguistic: Bantu-, Nilotic-, Nilo-Hamitic- and Hamitic-speaking peoples. The Kikuyu of the central highlands, part of the Bantu-speaking majority, are the largest tribe, comprising nearly half of the population; they enjoy considerable prestige and influence despite efforts to lessen their dominance. They are followed by the Luo, from the shores of Lake Victoria, and the Luhya of the western farmlands who make up another 25 percent. The Luo have developed a reputation as the country's leading intellectuals, and they hold many of the top university posts.

Kenya's most famous tribe is the Maasai, a group of tall, pastoral nomads who resist the encroachments of modern civilization. They guard their cattle herds with spears and wear their traditional red cloaks and bright jewellery.

Asians, Arabs and Europeans form a small but vital minority. The Indo-Pakistani communities who emigrated here during colonial times retain control over much of the country's retail businesses. Arab residents go back much further to the coastal settlements founded in the Middle Ages. Kiswahili is the *lingua franca* that ties them all together, though English is also an official language.

The land once ruled by the Europeans has been largely returned to African hands. But the colonial legacy is marked by the prevalence of the English language, customs and,

for want of a better word, cuisine. Vehicles drive on the left, and the structure of government and public services all show the abiding influence of British models.

Kenya is seen as an oasis of calm and stability on a continent that has known little but turmoil in the decades since decolonization. This image has **8** been a great advantage in at- tracting the tourist trade; indeed, tourism has become the mainstay of the economy, surpassing tea and coffee as the major foreign income earner. But recently, cracks have appeared in this veneer.

Much of the country's stability has been maintained through iron-handed rule. The elections of December 1992 (see p 19) provoked violent

*The flamingos at Lake Nakuru: one of the world's finest wildlife spectacles.*

More alarming threats come from outside Kenya's borders. The conflicts in neighbouring Somalia, Ethiopia, Uganda and the Sudan have spilled into the northern region, in the form of occasional bandit attacks and an influx of refugees. Outbreaks of poaching, though largely eliminated, sometimes flare up in some of the game parks. While these occurences seldom endanger the casual tourist, always follow the advice of the authorities when travelling in remote regions, and respect any no-go areas.

With an estimated 24 million people, half of whom are under the age of 15, Kenya has one of the highest rates of population growth in the world. Yet only about one quarter of the land is arable. With this equation, poverty threatens to become more visible and more

ethnic clashes in the provinces, and fears of political unrest kept many tourists away. These fears were unfounded, as Kenyans accepted the election results peaceably and got on with their daily affairs, preferring to restore equilibrium than to incite confrontation. The new opposition parties, however, continue to clamour for political change.

widespread. Yet, despite this, Kenya's social problems are not glaringly apparent.

What will strike you instead is the friendliness of the people, their ready smiles and easy-going nature. Outside the larger cities there is a genuine interest in visitors and delight in a casual chat. All along the road children wave and smile; even the fearsome Maasai will often raise a hand in greeting. The kids will beg a little: have a handful of writing pens or some souvenir coins from your

*Kericho's tea plantations produce Kenya's primary export crop.*

country to hand for those first few soft-hearted days.

When you go to Kenya, be prepared for an exciting sensory experience. You will have a trip here as you never had before, and you'll also come back keener, more alive and more demanding of your usual surroundings.

**10**

# A Brief History

East Africa has been called the 'cradle of mankind', and pre-historic man may well have taken his first footsteps across the savannah lands of Kenya. In 1972 a fossil skull was found at Koobi Fora on the shores of Lake Turkana; between two and three million years old, it is the oldest ancestor of modern man found to date. It now sits in the Nairobi National Museum, tagged with the simple moniker 'No. 1470'.

Some theories hold that the climate and topography of East Africa – particularly the rich, volcanic Rift Valley – provided the right environment for human evolution and that, over hundreds of thousands of years, these early ancestors migrated from this region to populate other continents. Whatever the case, some of the earliest remains of Stone Age man have been found in Kenya at sites on Rusinga Island, Hyrax Hill, Kariandusi and Olorgesailie.

Kenya's earliest societies were hunter-gatherers. Cattle-herding and agriculture emerged only around 1000 BC, according to historians. In fact, Kenya seems to have remained largely at a Stone Age level until about AD 1000, when signs of iron-smelting appeared, brought by Bantu-speaking tribes from the west and south. The gradual change from a hunting-and-gathering society to one of agriculture led to some rapid increases in population in the fertile areas of the highlands and the grazing plateaux of the south-west.

## Settlement of the Coast

Arabs landed on the Kenya coast in the 7th century AD, looking to develop trade between East Africa and the Orient. Later the rise of Islam in the Middle East caused a wave of migration to the coastal strip – a pattern which continued into the 12th century. The intermingling of these settlers from the Persian Gulf with the Bantu population gave rise to the mixed Bantu-Arabic language of Kiswahili. The Swahilis produced Kenya's first

*T*he Muslim women of Lamu cover themselves with the traditional black bui-buis.

written language, in Arabic characters. Though the Islamic influence was pervasive, Swahili culture was also affected by interaction with Asia and the Orient.

Over the next 300 years, the Swahili trading centres, scattered along the coastline, developed into powerful city-states: **12** Mombasa, Malindi and Lamu

were among the most dominant. They manufactured iron and ceramics, and traded with ships from Persia, India and the Far East, exchanging animal skins, ivory, tortoiseshell, gums and spices for sugar, grain and cloth. The coastal dwellers dealt mainly with the outside world, and had few links with the Kenya interior.

In 1498 Vasco da Gama, searching for a sea route to India, landed in Malindi. The Portuguese soon returned to plunder the rich coastal cities. While Mombasa fiercely resisted the encroachment, the Portuguese formed a trading alliance with its rival state, Malindi. Mombasa was attacked three times in the 16th century before surrendering to the Portuguese in 1592.

From their new military garrison at Fort Jesus the Portuguese reigned for the next century, but their hold was weakened by repeated native attacks and threats to their position elsewhere in the Indian Ocean and in the Gulf. In 1660 the Sultan of Oman supported a major revolt on Pate Island, north of Lamu. The Portuguese occupants were finally driven out of Mombasa in 1698.

Aided by British naval technology, the Omanis soon suppressed the Swahili rebellions and became the new foreign overlords on the coast. Ruling from their capital at Zanzibar, they cultivated the ivory trade with the interior; then, in the 1830s, a new trade, the slave trade this time, proved even more lucrative. By 1854 it had crossed over Kenya's borders into Uganda. Slavery was officially forbidden in 1873, but it took another 20 years for the illegal trade to cease.

## The Interior in Pre-Colonial Times

Prior to British colonization, Kenya's interior was populated by groups that took a long time to achieve tribal unity. Throughout this period there was a constant migration and merging of peoples now identified as Bantu-, Nilotic-, Nilo-Hamitic- or Hamitic-speaking. Tribal identity developed slowly, following the change from a pastoral to an agricultural way of life, and the subsequent fight for land ownership among neighbouring tribes.

The Maa speakers, namely the Maasai and the Samburu – were the last tribal group to arrive in Kenya. Gradually moving southward, within a few generations these obscure nomads had expanded along the plains and throughout the Rift Valley, to eventually become a strong force from Lake Turkana to Mount Kilimanjaro. Differences between Maasai groups erupted in the Maasai Civil Wars in the last half of the 19th century.

Political organization varied greatly among these various ethnic groups. The Bantus of north-western Kenya, for instance, did have a certain centralized organization, with a council of elders advising a clan leader paid for his services in meat, grain or beer. But the eastern Bantu people – most prominently the Kikuyu – were organized in peer groups known as age-sets, each serving a military, police or judicial function in ruling the **13** tribal lands. Solidarity came through kinship and territorial allegiance, rather than loyalty to a central council or chief.

Arab caravans from Mombasa ventured into the interior on ivory safaris, trading main-

*The Portuguese – and later the Arabs – ruled the coast from the stronghold of Fort Jesus.*

ly with the Kamba tribe. The quality of the ivory from Kenya's elephants was considered superior to that of their Indian cousins and sold better in the Orient. The caravans opened up routes from Mombasa to Kilimanjaro, across the Rift Valley to Lake Victoria and even as far north as Lake Turkana. The Arabs, however, were never able to gain a hold on the interior itself.

Missionaries and adventurers from Britain and Germany had moved upcountry as early as 1846, laying the groundwork for later colonization. Two of them, Johann Ludwig Krapf and Johann Rebmann – who worked for the British Church Missionary Society – located Mounts Kenya and Kilimanjaro; another – John Hanning Speke – 'discovered' Lake Victoria in 1858, whilst Joseph Thompson explored Maasai territory in 1883.

When the Europeans carved up the continent in the 1880s, Kenya, Uganda and Zanzibar went to the British and Tanganyika (Tanzania) to the Germans. Each monarch got a snow-capped peak: Mt Kenya for Queen Victoria and Mt Kilimanjaro for Kaiser Wilhelm.

## Under the Union Jack

The British colonized Kenya almost as an afterthought. They were, in fact, far more interested in their prospects in Zanzibar and Uganda. For several years, they left Kenya to the administration of the Imperial British East Africa Company, set up in 1888, who imposed taxes, built trading posts and pursued the ivory trade in the interior. Inept management of the territory forced the British government to take over the operation of what it called the 'East Africa Protectorate' seven years later.

A means of transport was needed between the coast and the source of the River Nile to reduce costs and develop plantation agriculture. In 1896 contruction began on a railroad line to connect Mombasa with Port Florence, today's Kisumu, which was later extended into Uganda. To pay for the high cost of the project, the government publicized the previously remote highlands as a great farming and settlement region. Immigrants from Britain, Europe and South Africa flooded in.

Lord Delamere, a pioneer agriculturalist, became champion of the white settlers. In 1903 he was given a grant of

*V*asco de Gama's pillar at Malindi commemorates the Portuguese landing in 1498.

**15**

40,000ha (98,840 acres) of rich farmland in the central highlands, north of Nairobi. Other settlers also appropriated huge landed estates for themselves, and introduced coffee, tea and pineapples. Cereals and other European crops also thrived, and this fertile region soon became known as the 'White Highlands'.

Within a few years, half of the prime farmland was controlled by the settlers. The Kikuyu were driven out and resettled on native reserves, where the growing population faced grave land shortages. Many had no choice but to work for the settlers as farm labourers and domestic servants. Colonial authorities imposed control by appointing tribal chiefs to collect hut taxes. A new class structure developed, as young Africans competed for wealth and privileges conferred by these chieftainships. One of the most hated laws required Africans to register and carry ID cards.

Apart from Swahili towns on the coast, Kenya's urban areas were all European in origin. Africans could work but not live there, except as 'sojourners' in shanty towns on the outskirts. Indians as well as Africans were denied farming rights in the White Highlands. In 1907 the capital of the protectorate was shifted from Mombasa to Nairobi, but it was not until 1920 that the region became known as the Crown Colony of Kenya, a name derived from the country's highest peak.

## African Ascendency

World War I had a profound effect on the 200,000 African soldiers who were conscripted into the British army. Living and fighting side by side in the campaign for Tanganyika, Kenyans learned military tactics and witnessed at firsthand the white man's real strengths and weaknesses. At the end of the war, the Soldier Resettlement Scheme rewarded the white servicemen with new land rights, while Kenyans returned to impoverished living conditions. This caused great bitterness, and a number of

*The Njemps, a small tribe related to the Maasai, live around Lake Baringo.*

political activist groups sprang up, made up chiefly of Kikuyu ex-soldiers.

The strongest group was the East African Association, led by a government clerk named Harry Thuku. At the peak of the protests in 1921, Thuku was arrested and thrown in jail for 11 years. Other militant groups, such as the Kikuyu Central Association – referred to as KCA – carried on the nationalist movement. It was known as *Uhuru*: the call for independence.

In the 1920s and 1930s, settlers in the White Highlands enjoyed an unprecedented heyday of good fortune. Meanwhile, the government tried to diffuse the clamour for independence by courting the more moderate among the African leaders. In 1944 Eliud Mathu was made the first African member of Kenya's Legislative Council. Moreover, he was also permitted to form an advisory group.

Just two years later, Jomo Kenyatta, one of the movement's first leaders, returned to Nairobi after 16 years of study and political activism in England. He took over Mathu's advisory group, renamed it the Kenya African Union, and set about to transform the small educated elite into a mass political movement open to all workers and war veterans.

However, differences grew between Kenyatta's radicals – **17** who sought independence through revolutionary methods – and the moderates surrounding Eliud Mathu who wanted a gradual, reformist approach. The moderates especially resented Kikuyu domination of the KAU, and Kenyatta agreed that multi-tribal leadership was essential to national independence, a problem that continued to plague him after independence was achieved.

## The Mau Mau

A radical underground movement arose when young Kikuyus took secret oaths against the British government, leading to guerilla attacks against settlers in the White Highlands. Known as the Mau Mau rebellion, the name is believed to have been derived from a Kikuyu warning that the enemy was approaching. A state of emergency was declared in 1952, and though the KAU did not participate in the attacks, Kenyatta and other leaders were jailed.

The fighting proved fierce. Thousands of Kikuyus, Embus and Merus were resettled in guarded areas. Finally, in 1956 British troops drove the Mau Mau bands into the Mount Kenya and Aberdare forests, where they were either killed or captured. The casualties of the rebellion numbered over 11,000 Mau Mau, some 2,000 African civilians, 50 British troops, and a total of 95 European settlers.

The armed rebellion was broken, but colonial authority was, finally, at an end. In 1960 the White Highlands, which cover 800,000ha (1,976,840 acres), were opened up to black ownership.

However, Kenya's tribal conflicts were still unresolved as the Kikuyu-dominated Kenya African National Union, abbreviated KANU, competed for power with the Kenya African Democratic Union (KADU) of the minority tribes. Kenyatta returned from exile to lead KANU in 1961. Independence was finally achieved on 12 December 1963, and when a Republic was proclaimed the next year, Jomo Kenyatta was named president.

## Independence

Kenyatta began his presidency under the banner of *Harambee*: 'pulling together'. His skill in transferring power to African hands, while courting the aid and support of the former colonial rulers, earned him the title of respect, *Mzee*, or 'Honourable Old Man', whilst Kenya emerged as a model of democracy and progress among African countries.

Following the election, however, the KADU opposition was dissolved and Kenya became a one-party state. There was growing corruption and internal unrest, but political dissent was squashed by persecution and the fear generated by the assassination of Tom Mboya, a Luo politician tipped to become the next president. Kikuyu dominance grew, and when Kenyatta died suddenly in August 1978, he did so as one of the world's richest men.

Daniel Arap Moi, a member of the minority Kalenjin tribe, was chosen to succeed Kenyatta in order to combat tribal rivalry between the Kikuyu and the Luo. His initial efforts to wipe out tribalism and corruption were well-received but short-lived. The next decade was marred by an attempted military coup in August 1982, accusations of internal plots against the government, student unrest and human rights violations.

Kenya had long enjoyed influxes of foreign aid, but during the early 1990s Western donors, alarmed at reports of widespread corruption and political repression, suspended further aid until the Moi government demonstrated progress on human rights and political reform. As a result, in late December 1992, Kenya held its first multi-party elections since independence. Unfortunately, the opposition parties which emerged were unable to form a united block to unseat Moi, who was re-elected amid accusations of vote-rigging and violent ethnic clashes in the provinces. However, the foundation has been laid for change as Kenyans continue to strive for stability, growth and prosperity.

**19**

# Where to Go

## Nairobi

### CENTRAL NAIROBI

In less than a century Kenya's capital, **Nairobi**, has grown from a remote railway outpost to become East Africa's largest city. Its modern skyline seems to announce its prominence as an international convention centre, a headquarters for multi-national businesses and United Nations bureaux, and, not least, the safari capital of the world. Kenya's political, administrative, business and trade activities are all centred in this town.

Nairobi has the attendant problems of capital cities everywhere: traffic, street crime and a rapidly growing population (last estimated at around two million), many of whom are poor. But for the thousands of visitors who pass through each year, eagerly preparing for the bush or resting up between safaris, the capital city is not an unpleasant place to be. At 1,660m (5,446ft) above sea level, the equatorial climate is temperate all year-round with warm, sunny days and cool nights. There are plenty of restaurants, shops, and service facilities, safe drinking water and few mosquitoes. Furthermore, in a country where hurry is nowhere considered a virtue, the central streets of the city almost bustle. Most first-time visitors will be unaware of the great contrasts that lie between the sprawling shantytowns to the east and the spacious, landscaped homes of the northern and western suburbs. Instead, they will notice the curious mixture of colonial legacy and African resurgence that makes up Nairobi.

In 1899, when builders of the Mombasa-Uganda railroad line established a supply depot at Mile 327, this bleak and swampy riverside place that the Maasai called *enkare nyarobe* (sweet water) was nothing more than a campsite for hundreds of Indian labourers. A few wooden shacks housed the engineers who paused here to

*The neo-classical City Hall in Nairobi, a landmark of the city, evokes Kenya's colonial past.*

contemplate the difficulties of laying track across the Great Rift Valley. Soon, a frontier town emerged, with a central street (now Kenyatta Avenue) broad enough for a 12-span oxcart to wheel around.

Three years later the place was nearly abandoned when plague swept the town, and a government decree had it burned to the ground. Despite another plague in 1904, Nairobi was rebuilt and by the time the Protectorate had officially moved its headquarters there from Mombasa in 1907, the white hunters were streaming **21** in to embark on safari from the newly opened Norfolk Hotel. The most prominent of them was Theodore Roosevelt, the US President, who headed a safari with 500 porters, all dressed in blue, and each carrying 25kg (55lb) of supplies. In ten months – while out of office – Roosevelt bagged no less than 296 animals.

Meanwhile, the British government was strongly encouraging settlement of the Central Highlands, and Nairobi became the social and commercial centre for the growing white farming community. Indian traders developed the bazaar, while Africans came in from the villages to work as labourers. During World War II Nairobi served as a major garrison town and much of the local game was killed to provide food for the troops. Thus, in 1947, the government formed the first of Kenya's many game sanctuaries, Nairobi National Park.

The building dominating the skyline, the **Kenyatta Conference Centre**, symbolizes the interaction of the city's European origins and African destiny by combining a cylindrical skyscraper that could just as easily be in London or Frankfurt, with a cone-shaped congress hall reminiscent of tribal huts. It's worth a trip to the top for the view of the city and the surrounding hills. A statue of Jomo Kenyatta sits alongside in City Square, as do the old neo-classical Law Courts, the very model of an English county court building.

White-columned arcades, the dominant architectural feature of the business district, are perfectly adapted to the climate, offering protection from the sudden rains or midday sun. They shelter the shops and restaurants along Mama Ngina Street – formerly Queensway and now named after Kenyatta's wife – and Kimathi Street, named after Dedan Kimathi, a Mau Mau leader executed by the British in 1957.

The Hilton Hotel, at the intersection of these two streets, is a focal point for foreign tourists. Across the road is the **Information Bureau**, a good place to enquire about transport and safari arrangements.

Two of the great traditional meeting places of Nairobi are the Norfolk and New Stanley hotels, which you can enjoy even if you are staying elsewhere. The **Norfolk**, in Harry Thuku Road, across from the university, is Nairobi's oldest hotel. The rickshaws in the garden were once used to ferry guests from the railway station. Have tea on the Delamere terrace or a gin and tonic in the bar with its caricatures of old colonial types on the walls, and you'll catch a whiff of the decades when the lion, the symbol of Kenya, had a Union Jack on its tail.

The **New Stanley**'s claim to fame is its Thorn Tree Café in Kimathi Street. Hunters and other travellers would leave messages pinned to the trunk of a huge acacia rising in the middle of the patio. Though the hunters have been replaced by tourists, and a brand new tree planted in 1961, the tradition remains: Franz tells Heidi (and the rest of us) that he'll meet her in Cairo, and Debbie tells Billy she won't be joining him in Marrakesh.

The long and broad Kenyatta Avenue, planted with flowering trees and shrubs, runs west from the New Stanley. A few blocks north along Muindi Mbingu Street, a rather more African hub of activity can be found around the **City Market**. You can browse through fragrant flower and produce stalls in the main hall, but remember to keep a tight hold on your valuables. The maze of curio stands offers good bargains on soapstone, wood carvings and other handicrafts – if you can endure the overbearing stallholders. Across from the market is the Arabian-style **Jamia Mosque**, built in 1933 by the Sunni sect.

Nearby Biashara Street – meaning 'business street' in Swahili – was called the Indian Bazaar in colonial times. You can still find everything you need in Biashara Street, from exotic swimwear to great safari suits.

The **National Museum**, on Museum Hill at the northern end of Uhuru Highway, deserves a visit above all for its great prehistoric collection **23**

*Ahmed, the great elephant from Marsabit, was declared a national monument.*

The remains of prehistoric animals include a giant ostrich, rhinoceros and elephant; on a smaller scale are extensive bird, insect and butterfly collections. As for exhibits on the rainforest and the Rift Valley, they'll provide a fascinating background if an excursion to these areas is on your itinerary – as do the artefacts from various tribes. In the museum courtyard is a stuffed model of Ahmed, the legendary elephant from Marsabit, who was declared a national monument by President Jomo Kenyatta in 1970 and placed under 24-hour honour guard to protect him from poachers. He died of natural causes four years later, aged around 60, with each magnificent tusk weighing an impressive 67kg (148lb).

depicting the origins of man and various animals. On exhibit here is a replica of No. 1470, the skull of our two-and-a-half million-year-old ancestor discovered at Lake Turkana. You can also view the findings from Olduvai Gorge in Tanzania: fossilized remains, 1,650,000 years old, of *Homo habilis*, the first tool-making man, with his stone hand-axes and cleavers; as well as *Homo erectus*, a 1,150,000-year-old man coming closer to the brain capacity of *Homo sapiens*.

Across from the museum is the **Snake House**, where you can safely view those creatures

**24**

you hope never to see in the wild: the deadly green mamba, black mamba, puff adder and red spitting cobra. These venomous reptiles have not dampened the sense of humour here: a sign above the snake pit states 'Trespassers will be poisoned', and visitors are informed that anyone throwing litter into the crocodile pond will be required to retrieve it.

## AROUND NAIROBI

Several other attractions are located on the outskirts of the city. If you are visiting Nairobi before you set off for the national parks and game reserves, a tour of the **Nairobi National Park** makes a good introduction. It has a beautifully varied landscape of forest, hills and savannah. Although Nairobi's well-marked, smooth-surfaced roads may seem a little tame if you've already

visited other parks, the sight of wildlife grazing majestically against the backdrop of the city skyline is still impressive. Good game viewing here is almost guaranteed.

There are lots of lions, and the gate keepers at the park entrance may tell you where they are to be found each day. While the park has no elephants, it does offer one of the best chances to see rhino, due to the black rhino sanctuary located here. Also look out for the ostriches (who do not bury their heads in the sand), warthogs, baboons, zebras, giraffes,

*C*rested cranes flaunt their delicate head-dresses at Nairobi National Park.

and impalas. Although the animals are fenced off on one side of the park from the Nairobi-Mombasa highway, they have free access for migration to and from Amboseli and Tsavo across the Athi and Kaputei Plains. If you have missed some of the animals at the other parks and reserves because they were too shy, you will find them so blasé about vehicles here they'll practically pose full-face, profile or rear view, as requested.

At the western end of the park is the **Animal Orphanage**, founded in 1963 to provide a home for young animals injured or deserted in the wild. Zoologists who care for them until they can be returned to the reserves have a chance to study these animals up close. It's a good place for children to have their first easy look at Kenya's wildlife, but for adults it may seem little more than a glorified zoo and has a fairly limited appeal.

En route to the park you will not fail to pass Kenya's majestic **National Independence Monument** in the Uhuru Gardens. It was erected on the site where the British government passed the papers of independence to the Kenyan people on 12 December 1963. A second monument marks the 25th anniversary of that day.

Nearby on Langata Road, you'll also find the **Carnivore Restaurant** where, after seeing the animals, you can go and eat them. Zebra, giraffe, eland, crocodile and other game meat is spit-roasted over a charcoal pit and carved on to hot pewter plates at your table. Do not despair, however: there is plenty of beef and chicken for the tender-hearted. A true experience, the restaurant is a favourite with both Kenyans and tourists and features on many tour itineraries.

The **Bomas of Kenya**, a couple of kilometres away, offers a chance to see traditional tribal dances performed by the Harambee Dancers, a professional dance group. Many find the 2-hour show – performed in a circular arena with an inferior sound system – way too long, but it does feature a variety of Kenyan dance styles and traditional instruments you'll be unlikely to see elsewhere. Still, if it proves too much, you can always go and explore the surrounding grounds, which are laid out with the traditional homesteads (*bomas*) of various tribes, and take time to peruse the arts and crafts for sale.

Another popular excursion is to the **Karen Blixen Museum**, the homestead where the author (pen name Isak Dinesan) lived and ran her coffee farm from 1917 to 1931. After the grandeur of the Hollywood film, *Out of Africa*, which was shot here, the first thing that strikes you about the house is how small it is. The beautiful wood-panelled rooms have been restored and filled with original artefacts and reproductions. From the pretty gardens you can gaze over the Ngong Hills where Karen Blixen's lover, Denys Finch Hatton, is buried.

The nearby **Langata Giraffe Centre** was founded in 1978 to save the Rothschild's giraffe from extinction. Though the aim of the centre is to teach schoolchildren about wildlife

*The National Monument in Uhuru Gardens commemorates Kenya's Independence Day.*

conservation, adults also enjoy the chance to hand-feed the resident giraffes as much as the kids do. **27**

# National Parks and Game Reserves

Every nation has its monuments and Kenya's are not cathedrals or palaces but rather the great wildlife that roams the length and breadth of the country. Animals and birds are accorded a privileged position and are protected against the wanton hunting and poaching that have nearly decimated many species. To name but one instance, the elephant population dropped from 165,000 in 1970 to 20,000 in 1988. That very same year, the number of rhinos, ruthlessly hunted solely for their horns, reached a low of 330.

In 1989 Dr Richard Leakey, world-renowed anthropologist and conservationist, took over as head of the Kenya Wildlife Service, or KWS. His efforts to eliminate poaching and improve both conditions and safety within the parks have been largely successful, enabling visitors to enjoy no less than 50 conservation areas comprising seven percent of the country's total land area. The most popular parks are Maasai Mara (see p.84), Amboseli (p.86), Lake Nakuru (p.56), Nairobi National Park (p.25) and Tsavo (p.88).

Protecting Kenya's wildlife is no small task. The parks are under intense pressure both from commercial developers and the growing population. Soil, trees and other vegetation that make up the eco-system must also be conserved for the animals to survive. Most parks in Kenya are not fenced, allowing game to migrate freely back and forth through transitional zones, but this natural order is becoming increasingly threatened as man and beast compete fiercely for the land and its resources.

KWS has begun a number of community wildlife programmes, whereby a portion of the gate takings at the parks is set aside for development projects in the adjacent areas, thereby enabling the local communities to see a direct benefit from wildlife conservation.

Kenya's national parks do not stop at the water's edge. A coral reef runs along nearly the entire length of the coast, and several marine national parks and reserves have been established to preserve this fascinating underwater ecosystem of live corals, tropical fish and marine animals.

Safaris – a Swahili word meaning 'journey' – are organized into the bush in jeeps and minibuses with pop-up roofs that allow wildlife viewing at close quarters – and some photography. Just after sunrise is the best time for a game run, before the animals settle down to rest in the heat of the day. Late afternoon is another optimum viewing time. Carnivores begin their hunt for dinner just before dusk, and it's the only time of day when the more camera-shy animals come out of hiding.

Game spotting is definitely an acquired skill, and the services of a driver or guide are invaluable; he can take you to the places most likely to shelter the more elusive animals, and provide useful informa-tion and folklore about the animals' habits. Keep on the lookout: animals have a natural camouflage, and without an experienced pair of eyes you may never notice that cheetah sinking slowly, slowly into the tall grass.

Topping most people's list of 'must see's' are the following Big Five: lion, leopard, rhino, elephant and buffalo. You will have many opportunities for photographing, filming and simply viewing with binoculars, but remember that safari is all luck. Keep in mind, however, as you read or hear about what species you can expect to see at this or that park, that they're not always to be found in the very same place. Animals migrate, weather conditions change and availability of food and water varies from day to day. During dry periods they tend to congregate around waterholes; after a rainy spell the vegetation is higher and denser, making the animals much harder to see.

It's better to relax and enjoy whatever the luck of the safari brings your way. **29**

## Do's and Don'ts in the National Parks and Game Reserves

You soon learn to accept the rules and restrictions operating in the parks and reserves as more than reasonable in the interest of preserving both the wildlife and natural beauty around you, as well as your own safety.

● Touring in the parks is permitted only during daylight hours – roughly 6am to an elastic 6pm. You very quickly get into a rhythm of early rising and early nights to take maximum advantage of the chances to see wildlife up close.

● You must enter or leave a park only at the designated gates. Pay your park fees willingly and remember the money is put to good use in maintaining all that you are here to see. Retain your ticket throughout your stay.

● Never drive through a park alone and always stay on the authorized roads and tracks. There are severe penalties for off-road driving as it destroys the natural habitat, disturbs the animals, and can even put you at risk. Driving too close to the animals is strongly discouraged; in all cases, keep a minimum distance of 15m (50ft).

● Never approach an animal – remember all park animals are wild. Do not try to lure them, or shout or honk your horn. Monkeys and other animals should not be fed or allowed to enter vehicles, rooms or tents.

● Driving speeds are limited to 40kph (25mph) inside the parks, but it is best to drive even slower than that. You will see more, disturb the animals less, and stir up less dust. Parks roads are deliberately left in their natural state; the potholes help to slow down traffic!

● It is important not to damage or destroy any vegetation; it is an important part of the animals' habitat. Do not throw cigarette butts out of the window, especially during the dry season.

● For your own safety, under no circumstances should you get out of your vehicle during a safari except at designated observation points. For this reason, it is all the more important to ensure that the vehicle you hire is in good working order and equipped with tow rope, jack and other useful tools.

If your car breaks down or you get stuck in the mud (and in the rainy season you most certainly will!) you cannot walk up the road for help – there are animals out there even if you can't see them. It helps to have a little food and drink on hand while you're waiting for help to come along.

● Be considerate of other park users who may want to view the wildlife in peace. Unnecessary noise and chatter can scare away the animals.

● In the marine parks, do not step on corals while snorkelling or diving. It is illegal to fish or take away any corals, seashells, or marine animals. Don't buy them, either, from any sellers on the beach; they will no doubt have been collected illegally.

# Who's Who in the Animal World

## Elephant
*(Tembo or Ndovu)*

Although the lion has long been regarded as the king of beasts, when you see animals working out their own hierarchy in nature, you are likely to conclude that the supreme monarch is the elephant. Certainly the lion himself makes way. You cannot fail to be impressed, even awed, by the prodigious nobility of elephants as they wander around in search of fresh grass, leaves or juicy bark, a cool waterhole or some mud to wallow in. You may also see them blowing dust over themselves with their trunks, then rubbing themselves against trees to remove ticks.

An adult male, 3m (10ft) tall, often weighs 5,400kg (11,905lb) and each tusk may weigh up to 90kg (198lb). The female, just under 3m, weighs a mere 2,700kg (5,950lb). But it is the females who do all the

*The majestic elephant; lions are lazy during the day and prefer to do their hunting after dark.*

work, are the leaders of herds and group their own baby and adolescent offspring and that of their daughters. Male elephants are chased away from the herd as soon as they are old enough to fend for themselves, at around 12 to 14 years, and join up with other males.

Enormously affectionate, the female elephants also do all the fighting to protect their young from lions and hyenas. The males turn up only when one of the females goes into heat. Pregnancy lasts up to 22 months, the longest of any mammal. Living till a grand old age of 50 to 60 years, elephants are known to bury their own dead and indeed other dead animals, even dead human beings they have killed: but, contrary to legend, they do not have mass burial grounds. (Indeed, when elephant skeletons have been found *en*

*masse*, it has been due invariably to mass killings carried out by humans encircling an elephant herd in a ring of fire.)

## Lion *(Simba)*

The lion is, arguably, the king of the jungle, though nobody would dispute that this is the most feared of African predators. Lions are ferocious hunters, but in the daylight hours when you will see them, they are more likely to seem docile, lazy, imperturbable and even downright friendly. Unless, of **33** course, they were unable to find a meal during the night, in which case their hunger might rouse them to action.

Lion prides, made up of several small families spread over a wide area, are more loosely knit groups than elephant herds. Lions roam over a territory that covers perhaps as much as 50sq km (some 20sq miles) in groups of threes and fours, usually lionesses with their cubs, while male lions tend to roam together, keeping separate from the females until mealtime.

With an arrogance that would enrage the mildest feminist, the male leaves almost all the hunting to the female and just waits for the kill, at which point he finally throws his weight around (a mere 180kg compared with the female's 110, or 295lb to 240lb), moves in, fights off the lioness and her cubs and takes... the lion's share.

In the male's defence, we can only say that his presence as a sentinel does keep the pride area safe for the lioness and her cubs.

The lion's favourite prey is zebra and buffalo. Both are big enough to provide a hearty meal for the whole family, but also strong enough, especially the buffalo, to require group effort to make the kill. Most antelopes can be knocked off single-handed.

Lions are extremely sensuous beasts. They like to lick, groom and rub up against each other, often as an act of group solidarity before the hunt or just out of good fellowship during the after-dinner siesta. Male lions are especially vain about grooming their opulent mane, their chief sexual selling-point. The roar, heard most often before dawn or early evening, is a crescendo of deep rolling grunts quite unlike that fabricated MGM groan.

## Baboon *(Nyani)*

Behaviourists have used the baboon as an analogy for theorizing about natural aggressiveness and male dominance among human beings. Quite apart from the dubious value of making such parallels, re-

**34**

*Grooming is an essential and often communal activity for baboons.*

You will often see male, female and baby baboons grooming each other. Their search for ticks, knots and dirt is an activity which reinforces group solidarity and what zoologists do not hesitate to call friendship. Male and female baboons form companionships independent of sexual mating. There is a definite hierarchy of prestige among female baboons, and the males seek some reflected glory by associating with the most prominent females – the troop's effective leaders who decide exactly when to move and which direction to take.

cent observations of baboons have shown them to be motivated not by fear and brutal tyranny, as had been claimed previously, rather by strong family relationships and social co-operation.

While the males play an important role in guaranteeing the safety of the baboon troop, it is the females who provide the group's stability. Females stay in the troop all their lives, while males are constantly on the move. Social cohesion is built around the family, with perhaps as many as 20 related units of mother and offspring. The males, for their part, form a separate band, moving on the outskirts of the group as it hunts for food.

The baboons' diet consists of young shoots of savanna grass, shrubs and herbs, but their favourite food is fruit, especially figs. They occasionally turn carnivore and hunt down birds, hare and young gazelles. Indeed, nothing would be safe on an unguarded picnic. **35**

Baboons, ever playful, are frequently naughty, even vicious when provoked, but a long way from being obnoxious criminals.

## Giraffe *(Twiga)*

In 1414 the Chinese Emperor was sent a unicorn as a gift through Arab traders in Malindi; but when it turned out to be a giraffe, he was reportedly not disappointed. Giraffes are the best argument for seeing animals in Kenya in their natural habitat, rather than in a zoo. You may think you already know what this weird beast looks like, but a delightful surprise awaits you when you finally spot one towering over the plain or decorously moving out between the trees on a hillside.

The giraffe has, it seems, achieved a state of grace, an ineffable dignity, just from being quite literally above it all – as much as 5m (16ft) for males. He relies on acute eyesight and his privileged vantage point to see potential dangers long before they arrive,

**36**

fleeing instead of coping with them in a fight. The giraffe gets his liquid from juicy or some dew-covered foliage, so as to avoid bending down to drink ground water in an ungainly split, vulnerable to attack from lions.

Females give birth standing up and the calf, already almost 2m (10ft) tall and weighing

*The reticulated giraffe of northern Kenya is the most distinctive of the three species.*

65kg (143lb), is dropped over a metre to the ground, head first and with a considerable thud. The fall breaks the umbilical cord. Freud would not be surprised to learn that this rude arrival on earth prepares the calf for a not very affectionate upbringing from the aloof female giraffe.

There are three main species: the reticulated giraffe, found only in northern Kenya, is bronze coloured with a distinct web-like pattern to its coat; the Maasai giraffe, which is smaller and darker with a ragged spot pattern; and the Rothschild giraffe, the tallest variety, whose coat pattern lies somewhere in between.

## Hyena *(Fisi)*

You're not supposed to like hyenas. With their oversized heads, sloped backs, scruffy fur and clumsy gait, they're ugly. They have a dozen ways to make a horrible din, including a whoop, a groan, a low giggle, yell, growl, whine as well as the famous blood-curdling laugh. And they have a miserable reputation as cowardly scavengers, waiting for other predators to do their hunting for them and feeding off the remains.

But field studies have revealed hyenas to resort much more to hunting than scavenging for their food. They hunt with considerable intelligence and courage, even attacking rhinoceroses and young elephants. Lions are stronger than hyenas; they often steal the latter's kill and actually rely much more on scavenging than the much maligned hyena.

Grouped in tightly knit clans of up to 20 members, they live in a den with entrance holes connected by a network of tunnels. They mark out the clan territory with their dung and go on regular border patrols to keep out rival clans. Unusual among the mammals, the females are stronger and heavier than the males (58 to the male's 54kg: 128 to 119lb). This evolution is thought to result from the mother's need to protect her young against the male's frequent cannibalistic tendencies.

**37**

Clan solidarity is constantly reinforced, particularly before a hunt, with some elaborate meeting-ceremonies: they will sniff each other's mouths, necks and heads, raise a hind leg and lick each other before going off, reassured, on the group activity. Hunting is a carefully co-ordinated affair.

Typically, hyenas will start to chase a herd of wildebeest (gnus) and suddenly stop again to take stock of the herd in motion. One of them spots a weakling and soon the chase resumes. They bring down the chosen victim with a series of well-aimed bites, bringing the whole unsavoury business to a swift end.

## Rhinoceros *(Kifaru)*

There is a certain sad poetry in the thought that the huge, lumbering, ill-tempered rhinoceros has a horn which the Orientals believe to have aphrodisiac properties. The historic and highly profitable quest for his horn has aggravated the poor rhino's temper. Other animals on the game reserves have gradually grown used to human beings, but every time a rhino sees us – and his tiny eyes don't see very well – he assumes we're after his blessed horn again.

The number of rhinos in Kenya have dwindled from 8,000 in the 1960s to fewer than 500 now. Although they

_Herds of zebras grazing in the open savannah are a frequent sight throughout the country._

and the other two slinking away. The rhino can move his 1,350kg (2,975lb) bulk up to 55kph (35mph), at least as fast as a lion, with an amazing ability to wheel suddenly to face an attack from the rear.

There's nothing remotely delicate about rhinos, not even their love making, which is accompanied by a lot of ferocious snorting and jousting resistance from the female before she finally submits. Unlike the few seconds expended by most animals, copulation between rhinos lasts more than 30 minutes and this is thought to account for the mythic properties attributed to that horn.

may move around in two's and three's, they tend to live alone.

There is nothing more desolate than the screaming groan of a solitary rhino disturbed by another at his waterhole. However, there is one creature that can approach the rhino with impunity: the little oxpecker (or tick bird) which perches on the rhino's back. In exchange for the rhino's ticks and flies, the oxpecker provides a loudly chattering alarm system to warn the sleeping rhino of any approaching danger.

Mother rhinos are ferocious defenders of their young. A concerted attack by three male lions on a rhino calf can result in one of the lions being killed

### Zebra *(Punda Milia)*

The big question is not how the zebra got his stripes, but why he bothered in the first place. The stripes don't act as **39** effective camouflage, nor are they a means of sexual attraction, since males and females have essentially the same coats – with sub-species ranging in colour from black and white to brown and beige. One theory holds that the stripes repel tsetse flies, another that the subtle individual variations of zebras' stripes enable them to recognize each other at a distance. But whatever the explanation, the optical effect of a couple of hundred zebras at full gallop is enough to make your head spin.

The herd consists of strong family units, in which a stallion stays together with up to six mares and their foals, and groups of male bachelors. The bachelor groups are quite frivolous, spending most of their time racing, wrestling and generally fooling around. Relations between the stallion and his 'harem' are cordial, enhanced by mutual grooming. If you have a nice striped coat, you keep it in good shape. Unlike many animals, the zebra stallion does not seem to fear being cuckolded and is most friendly and courteous to other stallions in the herd.

When lions or hyenas threaten, the stallion just stands his ground, biting and kicking the agressors to give his family plenty of time to escape. This ploy is quite often successful because lions prefer to rely on surprise attack, rather than a pitched battle, for making their kill. Hyenas, for their part, much prefer to tackle a weakling, rather than a stallion.

## Cheetah (Duma)

How do you tell a cheetah from a leopard? First, his body markings are round spots with pronounced black 'tear-marks' on the face, whereas the leopard's spots are like groups of five fingerprints and the face is spotted rather than 'tear-marked'. More importantly, if you get the chance to watch them, you will see the cheetah is much more lithe and elegant, and taller and slimmer than the leopard.

Cheetahs are not very gregarious, often hunting alone and so unable to protect their

*Though it ambles across the road at Tsavo, the cheetah is the fastest mammal on earth.*

kill when attacked by scavenging lions, hyenas or even vultures. A mother will dutifully rear her cubs and then part quite abruptly from them. They never acknowledge each other again. Male cheetahs fend for themselves, occasionally hunting with a couple of males, and meeting up with females only for mating – and then only after a fierce fight.

The mother's training of her cubs for hunting is a careful affair, as would befit the fastest mammal on earth: an amazing 112kph compared with the fastest racehorse's 77kph (70 to 50mph). At first the mother cheetah makes the kill herself, usually by biting through the prey's windpipe. The cub picks up the dead prey by the throat and 'strangles' it again. Gradually the mother lets the growing cub have first go at catching the prey, and only if he botches it will she intervene, so as not to risk losing the meal altogether. Alternatively, the mother makes the **41** first thrust and then leaves the weakened prey for the cub to finish off. When he reaches the age of 14 months, the cub is considered ready to do the job alone. Mother can go. You have a fair chance of seeing some of this, as the cheetah is the only big cat to hunt by day. Your best chance to witness this is in the early morning.

## Leopard (Chui)

Leopards are always described as elusive, and you will indeed be lucky to see one unless you happen to be in one of those game lodges that lure leopards to floodlit platforms with bait. Leopards keep to the cover of trees or dense undergrowth and their solitary, stealthy habits enable them to survive the attention of poachers much better than lions and cheetahs.

Females seem to roam at will, whilst male leopards are definitely territorial, staking out their home ranges by spraying urine along the boundaries and fighting off other males who might trespass. The big feline's usual roar sounds like wood sawing, but during mating it turns into a snarling and caterwauling reminiscent of alley cats, only ten times louder. Unlike cheetahs, the females make affectionate mothers and continue to meet up with their offspring, even after they've grown up and left home.

Leopards, like cats, are nocturnal beasts, spending the day resting in the shade, either under an overhanging hillside rock or up a tree, anywhere, in fact, where they can survey the surrounding countryside. Weighing between 35 and 55kg (75 and 120lb) on average, they are very powerful and versatile hunters, prepared to kill anything from small birds to animals as much as three times their size. Leopards can carry up to 45kg (100lb) of uneaten meat into the higher branches of a tree, out of the reach of scavengers. They particularly enjoy eating other carnivores such as foxes, jackals and serval cats, among others. This accounts for their notorious partiality for domestic dogs on occasions when they have wandered into town.

# The Central Highlands

The Central Highlands lie north of Nairobi, a fertile agricultural region whose highlights are Aberdare National Park and Mount Kenya. In colonial days European settlers took much of the best land here for themselves, and the area became known as the 'White Highlands' (see p.16). Today, however, the land is farmed by the native Kikuyu.

The drive north from Nairobi is a pretty one past thatched huts, lush slopes of coffee trees and passion fruit vines. If you happen to be travelling on a Tuesday or Saturday, stop by the colourful, open-air market at **Karatina**, about 20km (12 miles) before Nyeri, the centre of the region.

*The produce market at Karatina is one of the largest in Kenya, and well worth a visit.*

## ABERDARE NATIONAL PARK

The **Aberdare Mountains**, which form the steep eastern edge of the Rift Valley, were named after the Victorian president of the Royal Geographical Society, Lord Aberdare. Although the Kikuyu name, 'Nyandarua', has been officially restored, it has been slow to catch on. This impressive range is rich in wildlife and contains one of the country's largest protected forest areas.

Because of the dense vegetation, it is not always easy to catch sight of the animals while driving through the park. The best way to see them is to visit one of the purpose-built game viewing lodges. Guests are driven from a base hotel in Nyeri (The Outspan for Tree Tops or Aberdare Country Club for the Ark) to the forest lodges, where they can spend the night watching the parade of wildlife around a floodlit watering hole. The bedrooms are equipped with night alarms to announce the sighting of specific animals.

**Treetops**, on the eastern edge of the park, is the original 'tree hotel', literally built on stilts in a forest clearing. It started as a single cabin in 1932 for a few guests who would go there on moonlit nights to see the wild animals wander over to the waterhole and natural salt lick. Twenty years later,

*M*ajestic Kikuyu dancers perform in ceremonial garb at Thompson's Falls.

*R*oughing it in luxury with hot showers and electricity at Sweetwaters Tented Camp.

the expanded hotel welcomed Princess Elizabeth and the Duke of Edinburgh as guests, on their honeymoon. Out the night of their stay, news came of the death of King George VI and Elizabeth's ascension to the English throne. In 1954 Mau Mau rebels burned Treetops to the ground; it was rebuilt three years later on the other side of the waterhole.

**The Ark**, built to look like  Noah's vessel, lies at a higher altitude in the middle of the forest. Guests enter along a gangplank above the trees. The Ark is considered by many to be the better of the two for game viewing; lions frequent the waterhole and the elusive leopard and rare bongo are occasionally sighted here. At both lodges you are likely to **45**

see elephant, rhino, waterbuck, gazelle, giant forest hog and genet cats, among others.

Some 40km (20 miles) from Nyeri, on the slopes of the Aberdares, a different game-viewing experience awaits at **Sweetwaters Tented Camp**. Accommodation is in luxury tents (with hot showers, electricity and flush toilets) that ring one side of the waterhole. This set-up allows you to be out in the open air with the animals, protected by an electric fence that runs along a separation ditch.

The Sweetwaters camp is situated on a private game reserve, **Ol Pejeta**, which is part of a 18,015ha (110,000-acre) ranch that once belonged to

*M*orani, a tame rhino orphaned as a baby and raised in captivity, has a 24-hour guard at the Ol Pejeta Rhino Sanctuary, set in Aberdare National Park.

the arms billionaire Adnan Kashoggi. Ol Pejeta is a peaceful retreat on flat, open savannah land that is good for game spotting. The camp specializes in night game drives, which are no longer allowed in Kenya's national parks, and there is a rhino sanctuary on the reserve.

## Nyahururu

At 2,360m (7,742ft), Nyahururu (**Thompson's Falls**) is Kenya's highest town, lying almost on the equator. The waterfall here is named after the explorer Joseph Thompson, who discovered it in 1883. The falls are a popular stop-off point for tourists, though the 70m (230ft) cascade is pretty rather than dramatic, and the serenity of the surrounding forest is somewhat marred by the pestering of the curio sellers on the cliff ledge.

You can climb to the foot of the falls, but there is only one safe way down and occasional muggings have occurred on the path. The best plan is to enquire at Thompson's Falls Lodge for a guide.

## MOUNT KENYA NATIONAL PARK

Africa's second highest mountain, **Mount Kenya**, is an extinct volcano lying on the equator. On a clear day, you can see it for miles around, though its icy summit is often shrouded in mist. The snow-capped twin peaks – Batian at 5,199m (17,058ft) and Nelion at 5,188m (17,022ft) – were named after two Maasai ritual chiefs from the last century. Quite apart from its grandiose beauty, Mount Kenya is the exponent of a remarkable natural phenomenon. The German missionary-explorer Johann Ludwig Krapf was laughed at when he reported snowfields on the equator in 1849, but Joseph Thompson confirmed the phenomenon 34 years later. In fact, Mount Kenya is the only point anywhere around the globe to have continuous equatorial snow.

Mount Kenya's two highest peaks are regularly scaled by experienced climbers, though few make it to the very top. A third peak, Lenana, lying at **47**

4,985m (16,354ft) has become known as 'Tourist Peak' because it is a relatively easy climb. If you set off up the mountain, be prepared for the cold temperatures and precipitation of a high-altitude environment. The preferred entry point for a climb is Naro Moru, on the western side.

The walk is a botanist's delight. The dense forest changes to bamboo jungle at 2,500m (8,200ft) and then, at 3,000m (9,840ft) to clearings surrounded by charming Abyssinian Hagenia trees hung with orchids, old-man's beard and several other creepers.

But there are much easier ways to enjoy Mount Kenya, with **Mountain Lodge** lying at the south-western edge of the massif inside Mount Kenya National Park and offering the best spot for game viewing. This tree hotel sits right in the heart of the rainforest. Buffalo, antelope, elephant, and sometimes lion, leopard and rhino are among the visitors to the floodlit waterhole, while mischievous Sykes monkeys clamber along the roof and ledges (and occasionally into your room through an open door!). All the rooms have balconies overlooking the waterhole, and

*M*ount Kenya draped in mist (left). A scientific demonstration of a curious phenomenon on the Equator (below).

a night watchman will wake you without fail if one of the animals you have asked about appears. At 2,195m (7,200ft) nights are chilly, so do bring warm clothes.

North of Naro Moru you'll cross the equator just outside **Nanyuki**. You can't miss the yellow marker that proclaims 'This Sign is on the Equator', or the cluster of souvenir stalls. It's a mandatory photo stop, and you'll no doubt meet a chap with a funnel and a bucket of water who will demonstrate how water swirls clockwise down a drain north of the equator and anti-clockwise south of it.

The **Mount Kenya Safari Club** is a luxurious landmark on the mountain's northern side. In 1959 Hollywood star William Holden transformed a local hotel into an African retreat for the international jet set, with landscaped gardens, golf course, riding stables and a croquet lawn. If you can't splurge on a night here, treat yourself to the buffet lunch and marvel at this equatorial oasis set against the mountain backdrop. You can also visit the adjacent **Mount Kenya Game Ranch and Animal Orphanage**, which has successfully bred the rare African bongo, a forest antelope with brown and white stripes seldom seen in the wild.

**49**

# Samburu-Buffalo Springs

The **Samburu** and **Buffalo Springs National reserves** are the northernmost of the popular game parks. At 300sq km (116sq miles) the area is small by Kenyan standards. Its attraction lies in the beauty of the landscape and the concentration of wildlife, including several species not found outside this region.

The reserves are roughly a two-hour drive north of Nanyuki. The tarmac ends at Isiolo, a service town with a mixed community of native Borans and Somali Muslims. There is a police checkpoint at the end of town where you must register your destination and fend off the harmless but assertive jewellery sellers who besiege the tourist vans. The checkpoint is there to act as a safeguard against Somali bandits, called *shiftas*, who once waged a border dispute over Kenya's northern territory.

Once past the checkpoint, the bumpy dirt road enters the land of the **Samburu**, a pastoral tribe related to the Maasai. Tall and slender, they resemble the Maasai in native dress and decorative jewellery, and the hair of the warriors is styled with ochre-coloured clay. Several villages consisting of low huts made of woven branches coated with mud and sisal mats lie on the outskirts of the reserves, and you will see many Samburu tending their herds of goats and cattle. However picturesque they may appear, remember that they will expect payment from tourists for taking their photographs.

The Ewaso Nyiro River divides the two reserves, with Samburu on the north bank and Buffalo Springs on the south. No river in Kenya is free from crocodiles, and this one has its fair share of particularly large, impressive ones.

Barely 20 years old, Samburu National Reserve receives a steady stream of visitors and there are several upmarket lodges and a luxury tented camp for accommodation. The wild, acacia-dotted landscape surrounds Koitogor Mountain in the middle of the reserve, while the red granite outcrop of Lololokwe rises outside the northern boundary.

**Buffalo Springs** is named after the underground springs here, which were uncovered by the British army in the 1960s, when they blew out a 12m (40ft) wide hole. The natural pool created by this event is one of the few places in the reserve where you can get out of your vehicle and swim safely, making it a popular picnic spot. **Buffalo Springs Tented Lodge** is the only accommodation here outside the campsites, with permanent tents, cottages and bandas, and superb views across the marsh to the Wamba Mountains.

Animals migrate freely between the two reserves, as do the guests on their daily game drives. Of special interest is the **Grevy zebra**, which is larger than the common zebra, with trumpet-shaped ears and a white belly. It is not found outside northern Kenya, and nor is the reticulated giraffe, which roams the area in large numbers. The distinctive bronze,

*The graceful gerenuk is only found in the region of Samburu and Buffalo Springs.*

web-patterned coat and white markings of the reticulated giraffe make it the most handsome of the three varieties (see p.36). Other rare species endemic to this area include the **Beisa oryx**, the blue-legged (male) **Somali ostrich** and the **gerenuk**, also known as the giraffe gazelle because of its long neck, slender frame and its habit of standing on its hind legs to nibble at tree branches. **51**

# The Great Rift Valley

The **Great Rift Valley** is part of a geological fault that runs across Africa from the Zambezi Delta in Mozambique to the Jordan Valley. It was formed in the Pleistocene era when the collision of two parallel plates thrust the harder rock upwards while the softer rock dropped nearly 1,000m (some 3,280ft) to form a wide trench bottom. The resulting chain of lakes and extinct volcanic cones that run along the Rift Valley, as it cuts through the highlands and descends into the Maasai Plains, makes it Kenya's most distinguishing topographical feature.

Most tour itineraries feature a visit to one or two of the Rift Valley lakes, which stretch out along a north-south axis from Lake Turkana in the far north to Lake Magadi, which is completely dry and the source of the world's largest soda deposits. Those with a special interest in bird-watching should plan to spend a little more time in this area, as over 450 resident and migratory species have been recorded around the central lakes.

The lakes lie in the valley floor, surrounded by a fairly tame landscape of farmland in the south and overgrazed scrubland further north. There are several good viewpoints overlooking the Rift Valley – particularly the one facing the dormant volcano, Mount Longonot – along the eastern escarpment on the main road north from Nairobi. The most dramatic landscape, seemingly more characteristic of the Rift Valley's turbulent past, is along the C51 highway between Marigat and Eldoret. It climbs through the pretty sculpted shapes of the Tugen Hills to Kabarnet before dropping down sharply through the Kerio Valley and back up again along the high, twisted roads and spectacular vistas

*Mount Longonot towers above the small farming plots of the Great Rift Valley.*

of the Elgeyo Escarpment. At Iten the scenery and road conditions change abruptly as you cross a high plateau to Eldoret.

## LAKE NAIVASHA

The closest lake to Nairobi, **Lake Naivasha** is as much a weekend retreat for city residents as a stop-over for tourists. At 1,890m (6,201ft) it is the highest of the Rift Valley lakes. The reed-rimmed shoreline, with its floating clumps of papyrus, changes constantly with the fluctuating water level. You can fish for black bass and tilapia, but the main attraction of this freshwater lake is its birdlife, which is best observed on a boat trip to the wildlife sanctuary on Crescent Island. The island is actually the outer rim of a volcanic crater that forms the deepest part of the lake.

Here, as at all of Kenya's lakes, take extra precautions against mosquitoes from dusk to dawn. The mighty, yellow-barked acacias around the lake

were called 'fever trees' by the early settlers who thought they were somehow responsible for malaria. In fact, both the trees and mosquito larvae thrive near large bodies of water.

Formerly Maasai country, the heavily irrigated, agricultural land around the lake is still largely owned by Europeans and is used to grow vegetables, carnations and other flowers, primarily for export. The Naivasha vineyards, the country's one and only commercial wine-growing area, are located on the southern shore.

## HELL'S GATE NATIONAL PARK

A few kilometres down the road is **Hell's Gate National Park**. Though small in area – 68sq km (26sq miles) – the landscape is impressive, with some spectacular rock formations and steep, fiery basalt cliffs enclosing vast stretches of open grassland. This is one of the few parks where you can leave your vehicle and explore the area on foot. The volcanic pinnacle called Fischer's Tower,

named after an early German explorer, marks the entrance to the gorge. There is a warden's post and information centre about 11km (7 miles) in from the Elsa Gate, where a nature trail leads to Ol Basta, a second volcanic plug. The clouds of steam emitted from the adjacent ridgetop mark the Olkaria Geothermal Station.

Although they have not been spotted for several years, a pair of rare **lammergeier eagles** once numbered among the many raptors nesting in the cliffs. Giraffe, impala, hartebeest, zebra and Grant's and Thomson's gazelle all graze in the grasslands among the whistling acacia thorn bushes, along with buffalo and the majestic eland.

## LAKE NAKURU

**Lake Nakuru** is famous for the multitude of **flamingos** that flock here to feed on the algae. The lake has no outlet and so minerals build up, giving the water a high alkaline content. Algae thrive on it, and so in turn do the flamingos.

## Relics from a Bygone Age

If you are interested in Kenya's prehistoric beginnings, you might like to stop on your way up to Nakuru at the Stone Age sites of Kariandusi and Hyrax Hill.

At KARIANDUSI, you can see examples of obsidian handaxes and cleavers and some fossilized bones. (Kariandusi is a palaeolithic campsite perhaps as much as 400,000 years old.)

HYRAX HILL is probably the more interesting of the two sites. A neolithic village of pit dwellings, dating from about 1000 BC, and a later Iron Age cemetery, in which skeletons were found, are visited on the guided tour. You can also make the climb – fairly strenuous in the midday heat – to the top of the hill fort for a view of the nearby lake and the jacaranda trees of Nakuru town. Utensils and other artefacts found in the graves are on view at the small museum.

On the hillside, you'll come across a version of the famous *bao* game, still played throughout Africa, cut right out of the rock. It consists of two parallel rows of small cavities in which pebbles are transferred from one to another until captured by one of the two players.

In earlier years up to two million birds would mass here at one time, covering the entire surface of the lake and creating what has been called 'the world's finest wildlife spectacle'. In the late 1970s, however, a period of exceptionally heavy rainfall raised the water level, causing a corresponding decrease in the water's alkalinity. The flamingos dispersed to other lakes in the Rift Valley, primarily Lake Bogoria. When the lake receded to its original size, the birds failed to return in their earlier numbers. Nevertheless, many thousands can usually be seen spreading out in a dainty pink ribbon along the shoreline.

There are two main species: the Greater Flamingo – taller and whiter – and the Lesser **55**

Flamingo, which is unique to the Rift Valley and greatly outnumbers its larger cousin. The pink hue of the flamingo's white feathers is caused by a carotene pigment in the algae. A large number of pelicans also fish for tilapia in the lake.

## Lake Nakuru National Park

**Lake Nakuru National Park** surrounds the lake, a mixed landscape of acacia woodland and rocky cliffs. It provides a habitat for over 400 species of bird, lion, leopard, jackal and Rothschild's giraffe, among many others. Black rhino have been translocated from other parts of the country in the hope that they will breed successfully to restock other national parks. To protect them from poachers, an electric fence has been erected around the park's entire perimeter.

Watch out for the huge pythons which inhabit the dense woodland areas between the lakeshore and the cliffs. Hippo Point boasts a far less threatening group of hippos. In addi-

tion, the picnic site at the top of the Baboon Cliffs offers a panoramic view looking out across the lake.

## LAKE BARINGO

The northernmost of the central Rift Valley lakes, **Baringo** is a freshwater lake with abun-

*F*ischer's Tower (left) marks the entrance to Hell's Gate National Park. Waterbuck and flamingos at Lake Nakuru (above).

dant stocks of tilapia, catfish and other colourful vertebrates. The cloudy, brown colour of the water comes from the large deposits of topsoil washed down the river during the rains; this erosion also accounts for its shallowness – throughout all its 168sq km (65sq miles) it is no deeper than 12m (39ft).

Hippos wallow throughout the lake and graze on its shore at night, often wandering on to the lawns of the **Lake Baringo Club**, the only lodge on the lakeshore. Crocodiles are also numerous but do not reach any great size.

With 470 species recorded around the lake, the area is a **bird**-lover's paradise. Gibraltar Island has the largest nesting colony of goliath herons, the tallest of the species at 1.5m (5ft). Herons, Verreaux's eagle, great white egrets, and a wide variety of hornbills are other star attractions. A resident ornithologist at the lodge leads morning birdwalks along the nearby escarpment and evening walks along the lakeshore. You may ask him all about the local winged residents. **57**

Hour-long boat trips out on the lake are available at the lodge, but they're pricey. You can get a longer (though no cheaper) trip from William at the Fish Factory, just down the main road past the campsite. He'll whistle for the fish eagles who swoop down from the island cliffs to snatch up a fish, an exciting sight. You'll also see hippos, herons, monitor lizards and other wildlife on the shores of the islands.

You can make another excursion to a Njemps village, a small tribe related to the Maasai, where you'll see the lifestyle of a man, his three wives and 18 children. For once, you can take as many photographs as you like.

## LAKE BOGORIA

After driving through a barren, sun-baked landscape broken only by scrawny goats scavenging along the roadside and red termite mounds rising like sand castles between the bushes, the blue waters of **Lake Bogoria**, lying to the south of Lake Baringo, may well seem like a mirage. Early explorers who discovered it on their way to Uganda described it as the most beautiful view in Africa, and, indeed, the sight of Bogoria's steaming geysers set against the backdrop of the lake's rocky precipices is quite magnificent.

A local legend claims that the lake was formed when the god Chebet, angered by the stinginess of the Kamale tribe towards passing travellers, invoked a deluge which lasted for days and wiped out their village. Lake Bogoria is still

called 'the place of the lost tribe', and campers who have slept here overnight claim to have heard the wailing of the lost Kamales who perished in the flood.

While the steaming springs may well look like the fury of the gods, they are actually the remnants of past volcanic activity. You can get out of your car for a closer look at the **sulphurous pools** which bubble like a cauldron. Brave picknickers have been known to boil their eggs in the water. However, great care should be taken when walking near the springs, as the earth's crust is very thin, with scalding water simmering just below the surface. This area is very remote,

*T*wo awesome sights you'll come across in the Rift Valley: termite mounds rising amid the dry scrublands (left), and the steaming geysers and bubbling thermal pools of Lake Bogoria (below).

and it's a long way to the nearest burn unit.

Like Lake Nakuru, Bogoria's waters are alkaline, and if you haven't seen many **flamingos** at Nakuru, you'll probably find them here. Bogoria has outdistanced Nakuru in the flamingo count in recent years, with up to half a million gathering at a time. Over 350 other bird species have also been recorded here.

Lake Bogoria is the best place in Kenya to catch sight of the **greater kudu**, a rare antelope with white stripes and long, spiral horns that was nearly wiped out by rinderpest disease in the last century. In 1973, a 107sq km (41sq mile) area around the lake was designated a national reserve, largely for their protection. Among other animals here are cheetah, hyena, jackal and leopard.

Special kudu game drives and bird-watching tours can be

arranged at the newly opened Lake Bogoria Hotel, which you will find just outside the Loboi Gate. In addition, there are three campsites on the southern side of the lake.

*A crop of tall sunflowers brightens a Luhya village in Western Kenya.*

# Western Kenya

Western Kenya is not a common destination on the tourist trail. But for the return visitor to Kenya, or maybe for those who have the time and the interest to look beyond the game parks and beach resorts, it offers an amazing diversity of environments, from swampland to mountain wilderness,

equatorial rainforest and the sultry shores of Lake Victoria.

Much of western Kenya is heavily populated, with fertile farmland and several small, busy market towns. The bulk of Kenya's tea plantations and sugar cane fields are located in this region. The Luo are the largest ethnic group, occupying the lowlands along the lake-shore, followed by the Luyha in the area north of Kisumu, the Nandi around Eldoret, the Kipsigis in the Kericho district and the Gusii in the Kisii hills.

Dusty, noisy **Eldoret** is one of the fastest growing towns in Kenya. There is little to do or see here, but the tourist class hotels, banks and post office make it an adequate stop-over en route to more interesting places in the area.

## SAIWA SWAMP NATIONAL PARK

Kenya's smallest national park, **Saiwa Swamp**, is well worth a visit to admire the unique ecological habitat confined within its 200ha (500 acres). The **62** park was created in 1984 to protect the **sitatunga** (pronounced 'statunga'), a semi-aquatic antelope that is only found in this area. This small, reddish-brown creature spends most of the day submerged in the water with only the tip of its nose sticking out. It emerges to feed in the early morning and late afternoon, dipping down again at the slightest inkling of danger. You can spy on the elusive sitatunga from the cover of a tree-hide overlooking the swamp (simply follow the signs for observation platform 4).

The boggy terrain is caused by the run-off from Mount Elgon. You can easily explore the **trails** in two to three hours and in normal footwear, as walkways and bridges have been built over the swamp. It is a delightful walk through indigenous rainforest. Vervet, colobus and the white-bearded de Brazza monkeys crash through the high branches overhead. From the five observation towers, you can look out over the swamp and catch sight of the many bird species, which number over 300.

# MOUNT ELGON NATIONAL PARK

**Mount Elgon** has been called 'Kenya's loneliest park', and this extinct volcano straddling the Ugandan border is indeed remote. Lower than Mt Kenya but with greater bulk, it has similar vegetation and wildlife. The south-eastern slopes of the mountain actually fall within the boundaries of Mount Elgon National Park.

During the rainy months, the roads are impassable and the upper slopes are hidden in clouds, making December to March the best time to visit. For those prepared to make the journey, the rewards are great: impressive cliffs, hot springs, mountain streams, massive trees and dense forest provide some of the best hiking in the whole of Kenya. A climb to Koitoboss Peak and the hot springs at Suam Gorge (which lie in Uganda) is also possible.

The main attraction for most visitors, however, is the **elephant caves** – the most famous of which is Kitum – located on the lower slopes inside the park. These huge caves extend horizontally into the mountain and are thought to have been carved out by elephant tusks. Amazingly, the giant pachyderms make their way up the rocky forest slopes to gouge lumps of sodium from this massive, natural salt lick. You can see the tusk marks on the cave walls. If you arrive early in the morning, you may still be able to catch some animals using the salt licks before they retreat into the forest. When walking up to the caves, keep an eye out for any buffalo or giant forest hogs which may pose a danger, and take care when entering the caves themselves. Should you wish to explore the depths of the caves, you will need a strong torch; the scores of fruit bats hanging on the roof are harmless.

Because of Mount Elgon's remote position on the Ugandan border, there have been security problems in the past with armed rebels and elephant poachers. Although things have calmed down in recent years, it is a good idea to assess the situation locally before setting **63** ff up the mountain. You will be safe enough in the park itself, as rangers at the gate will be able to offer advice and an escort if necessary.

## KAKAMEGA FOREST RESERVE

**Kakamega Reserve**, situated north of Kisumu, is Kenya's only equatorial rainforest. Once part of a vast, continental tract that stretched to the Atlantic Ocean, the 238sq km (92sq mile) reserve now attracts both nature experts and scientists as well as tourists to explore this isolated environment, one which no longer exists elsewhere in East Africa. A good guide can help you make the most of your visit by explaining the forest eco-system and identifying some of the unique trees and plants found here, as well as the resident wildlife. Colourful butterflies and some 330 different bird species have established themselves here, including the great blue turaco and crowned eagle.

### Rusinga Island

Rusinga is the best-known of Lake Victoria's small islands. A wealth of prehistoric fossils have been found here, including Mary Leakey's discovery of the skull *Proconsul africanus*, an early man-like ape.

Rusinga was also the birthplace of one of Kenya's greatest statesmen, Tom Mboya. A Luo politician beloved by many Kenyans, he was assassinated by Kikuyu gunmen in 1969 to the detriment of the entire country (see p.19).

You can reach the island by ferry or overland via a new causeway. Alternatively, take a flying safari, operated by African Explorations and Lonrho Hotels. You'll be flown from your nearest airstrip for a half-day fishing trip or overnight excursion at the Rusinga Island Fishing Club. The largest Nile perch caught to date weighed 92kg (203lb) – the boat trip across the lake is great fun even if you don't like to fish.

# A Selection of Hotels and Restaurants in Kenya

# Recommended Hotels

Kenya offers a range of accommodation to suit every pocket and preference. In between the luxury hotels, the safari lodges and the basic *bandas* are reasonable, comfortable establishments that won't cost the earth, but may be lacking in facilities. Prices vary tremendously, even within the same accommodation at different times, and a star rating is not necessarily a guide to price, nor is a price guide indicative of facilities. Our rating is therefore based on quality of facilities available, rather than price alone. Enquire at your travel agency for prices.

    I    basic accommodation

   II   comfortable accommodation, some facilities

 III  excellent accommodation, good facilities

## ABERDARES

### Aberdare Country Club   III

*Lonrho Hotels Kenya Ltd*
*PO Box 58581, Nairobi*
*Tel. (02) 216940, fax 216796*
Lavish highland hotel. Gourmet food, swimming, golf, tennis, fishing, horseback riding. Large wildlife sanctuary with nature trails.

### The Ark   III

*Lonrho Hotels Kenya Ltd*
*PO Box 58581, Nairobi*
*Tel. (02) 216940, fax 216796*
Well known upmarket tree hotel with four game-viewing areas and a photographic bunker. Single and double cabins, all en suite. For more details, see p.45.

### Sweetwaters Tented Camp   III

*Lonrho Hotels Kenya Ltd*
*PO Box 58581, Nairobi*
*Tel. (02) 216940, fax 216796*
Luxury resort featuring game viewing. Formerly the private game reserve of Adnan Kashoggi. 25 twin tents, en suite with hot water and electricity. Pool, horseback and camel rides, rhino sanctuary, night game drives, nature walks.

### Treetops   III

*Block Hotels*
*Central Reservations Office,*
*PO Box 47557, Nairobi*
*Tel. (02) 335807, fax 340541*
The original tree hotel, built among Cape chestnut trees (see p.44). 73 rooms, central facilities.

## AMBOSELI NATIONAL PARK

### Amboseli Lodge and Kilimanjaro Lodge ▮▮▮

*c/o Kilimanjaro Safari Lodge*
*PO Box 30138, Nairobi*
*Tel. (02) 338888*
Tourist class lodges; pleasant and well-equipped.

### Amboseli Serena Lodge ▮▮▮

*Serena Lodges and Hotels*
*PO Box 48690, Nairobi*
*Tel. (02) 710511, fax 718103*
Highly rated lodge. A stream runs through the dining room. 96 rooms grouped together like a Maasai village.

### Ol Tukai Lodge ▮

*Aardvark Safaris Ltd*
*PO Box 49718, Nairobi*
*Tel. (02) 331718*
Self-service lodge; reasonably priced, well-equipped *bandas*.

## LAKE BARINGO/ LAKE BOGORIA

### Island Camp ▮▮▮

*c/o Let's Go Travel*
*PO Box 60342, Nairobi*
*Tel. (02) 213033-7, fax 340331*
Luxury tented camp. Island Camp benefits from a fantastic setting on Olkokwa Island on Lake Baringo. Swimming pool plus all kinds of watersports: water-skiing, wind-surfing, canoe and kayak trips, as well as nature and bird walks.

### Lake Baringo Club ▮▮▮

*Block Hotels*
*Central Reservations Office*
*PO Box 47557, Nairobi*
*Tel. (02) 335807, fax 340541*
Only lodge on the lakeshore. Bird-watching with resident ornithologist, boat trips, swimming pool.

### Lake Bogoria Hotel ▮▮

*PO Box 208*
*Menengai West*
*Tel. (037) 42696, fax 40896*
Comfortable new hotel, about 5 minutes' drive from the reserve. Dining room, bar, pool and natural warm springs pool; 4 cottages, game drives.

## BUFFALO SPRINGS

### Buffalo Springs Tented Lodge ▮▮

*African Tours & Hotels*
*PO Box 30471, Nairobi*
*Tel. (02) 336858*
*Fax 218109*
Choice of cottages, *bandas*, round-evals and tents with shower and toilet. Lounge, bar, swimming pool. Great views.

**67**

## DIANI BEACH

### Diani Reef Hotel
*PO Box 35*
*Ukunda*
*Tel. (01261) 2624*
Seven restaurants, seven bars and casino.

### Leopard Beach
*PO Box 34, Ukunda*
*Tel. (01261) 2110/1*
Chui Grill, Bellevue Café, room service, mini bar. Floodlit tennis court, sports and watersports facilities, open-air disco.

### Neptune Village
*PO Box 83125, Mombasa*
*Tel. (01261) 2350/2353*
*Fax (01261) 2354*
40km (25 miles) south of Mombasa, Situated on a vast, unspoilt beach. 95 sea-facing rooms set in bungalows of four rooms each. Pool, sundeck, bars, live bands, tennis, sports, games, boutiques.

### Tradewinds Hotel
*African Tours & Hotels*
*PO Box 30471, Nairobi*
*Tel. (02) 336858, fax 218109*
Lovely Arab-style buildings set amid the palm trees. Dining room, bar, lounge, swimming pool, diving school. African barbecue on Saturday nights.

## ELDORET

### New Wagon Wheel Hotel
*Elgeyo Road, PO Box 2408,*
*Eldoret*
*Tel. (0321) 322753*
Recently renovated hotel providing reasonable accommodation.

### Sirikwa Hotel
*Elgeyo Road, Eldoret*
*Tel. (0321) 31655/67*
*Bookings: African Tours & Hotels*
*PO Box 30471, Nairobi*
*Tel. (02) 336858, fax 218109*
Large, comfortable hotel with bar, restaurant, swimming pool.

## MOUNT ELGON

### Mount Elgon Lodge
*c/o Msafiri Inns*
*PO Box 42013, Nairobi*
*Tel. (02) 330820/229751/223488*
*Fax (02) 227815*
Low tariffs. Ideal base to explore the mountain.

## KABARNET

### Kabarnet Hotel
*African Tours & Hotels*
*PO Box 30471, Nairobi*
*Tel. 336858, fax 218109*
Swim. pool, good food, plenty of room; good views from the roof.

**68**

## KAKAMEGA

### Golf Hotel

*Bookings: c/o Msafiri Inns*
*PO Box 42013, Nairobi*
*Tel. (02) 330820/229751/223488*
*Fax (02) 227815*

Classy accommodation with swimming pool, restaurant, bars, private airstrip, sports club and a golf course. Wonderful views of Mount Elgon and the Bunyore Hills.

### Kakamega Rest House

*Bookings: c/o The Chief Forester*
*PO Box 88, Kakamega*

Guest house built on stilts. Extremely basic accommodation. Bring your own food. A stay here allows you to see the forest at its best: in the early morning.

## MOUNT KENYA NATIONAL PARK

### Mount Kenya Safari Club

*Lonrho Hotels Kenya Ltd*
*PO Box 58581, Nairobi*
*Tel. (02) 216940, fax 216796*

Brainchild of the late American film star William Holden. Exclusive, expensive holiday resort. 70 suites, 12 cottages, 3 villas. Superb food. Heated swimming pool, golf course, tennis, horseback riding, croquet lawn, aviary.

### Mountain Lodge

*African Tours & Hotels*
*PO Box 30471, Nairobi*
*Tel. (02) 336858, fax 218109*

Rustic tree hotel on the slopes of Mount Kenya. Dining room, lounge. En suite bathrooms and balconies overlooking the waterhole.

## KERICHO

### Kericho Tea Hotel

*Box 75, Kericho*
*Tel. (0361) 30004/5*
*Bookings: c/o Msafiri Inns*
*PO Box 42013, Nairobi*
*Tel. (02) 330820, fax 227815*

Former Brooke Bond clubhouse with original 1950s furnishings, swim. pool, lovely gardens; comfortable, reasonably priced. Guided tours of tea estate and processing factory with advance notice.

### Mid-West Hotel

*Box 1175, Kericho*
*Tel. (0361) 20611, fax 20615*

Adequate accommodation and a restaurant.

## KISUMU

### Imperial Hotel

*PO Box 1866, Kisumu*
*Tel. (035) 41485, fax 40345.*

Rooms, self-service apartments, penthouse suites; restaurant.

**69**

## Lake View Hotel
*PO Box 1216,*
*Alego Street, Kisumu*
*Tel. (035) 45055/3141*
Reasonable hotel, a short walk
from the railway station.

## Hotel Royal ▯▯
*PO Box 1690*
*Jomo Kenyatta Highway*
*Kisumu*
*Tel. (035) 40336/7*
Charming, if a little run down.
Restaurant and swimming pool.

## Sunset Hotel ▯▯
*PO Box 215, Kisumu*
*Tel. (035) 41100/4*
*Bookings: African Tours & Hotels*
*PO Box 30471, Nairobi*
*Tel. (02) 336858, fax 218109*
Overlooking Lake Victoria. Locat-
ed in the southern affluent suburb,
a short taxi ride from centre. Large
swim. pool.

## LAMU

## Island Hotel ▯▯
*PO Box 179, Shela, Lamu Island*
*Tel. (0121) 3100*
*or book through:*
*Island Ventures*
*PO Box 70940, Nairobi*
*Tel. (02) 229880*
Situated in centre of Shela, a tradi-
tional fishing village, 3 minutes

from the beach. 14 rooms with private bathrooms. Watersports, dhow
trips to Manda Island. Rooftop
restaurant.

## Peponi Hotel ▯▯▯
*PO Box 24, Lamu*
*Tel. (0121) 3029/3154*
Highly acclaimed hotel at Shela
beach. Closed May and June. 26
rooms. Reservations necessary.

## MAASAI MARA
## NATIONAL RESERVE

## Cottar's Camp ▯▯
*PO Box 44191, Nairobi*
*Tel. 882408/227930*
Built near acacia and fig trees,
close by a natural spring. Arranges
foot safaris or night game drives.

## Governor's Camp and ▯▯
## Little Governor's Camp
*PO Box 48217, Nairobi*
*Tel. (02) 331871/331041*
*Fax 726427*
Superb old-style lodges on oppo-
site sides of the Mara River and
surrounded by attractive forest.

## Keekorok Lodge ▯▯▯
*Block Hotels*
*PO Box 47557, Nairobi*
*Tel. (02) 335807, fax 340541*
Oldest lodge, in the centre of the
park. Luxury accommodation.

## Kichwa Tembo

*Windsor Hotels*
*PO Box 74957, Nairobi*
*Tel. (02) 217497/217499*
*Fax 217498*
The 'Elephant's Head' is a luxury tented camp at the foot of the Oloololo escarpment. Good food.

## Mara Safari Club

*Lonrho Hotels Kenya Ltd*
*PO Box 58581, Nairobi*
*Tel. (02) 216940, fax 216796*
Forty luxury tents with four-poster beds, along the Mara River. Swimming pool, good food, lounge, resident naturalist, balloon safaris, airstrip.

## Olkurruk Mara Lodge

*African Tours & Hotels*
*PO Box 30471, Nairobi*
*Tel. (02) 336858, fax 218109*
Designed like an African village with comfortable thatched-roof *bandas*, the lodge sits atop the Oloololo escarpment with fantastic views over the Mara Plains where *Out of Africa* was shot.

## MALINDI

## Blue Marlin

*PO Box 54, Malindi*
*Tel. (0123) 20440*
Malindi's first hotel, built in 1934; Ernest Hemingway drank in the bar. Luxurious grounds, two swimming pools, lounge, good food.

## Driftwood Beach Club

*PO Box 63, Malindi*
*Tel. (0123) 20155*
Relaxed, unhurried atmosphere. Speciality: seafood cuisine.

## Eden Rock

*PO Box 350 Lamu Road, Malindi*
*Tel. (0123) 20480*
Good facilities, private beach.

## Lawfords

*PO Box 20, Lamu Road, Malindi*
*Tel. (0123) 20440*
Good average hotel in attractive coastal town.

## Silversands Hotel

*PO Box 91, Malindi*
*Tel. (0123) 20385/20842*
Modest , quiet holiday retreat, featuring a restaurant, a swimming pool and an uncrowded beach.

## MOMBASA

## Hotel Hermes

*PO Box 98419*
*Msanifu Kombo Road, Mombasa*
*Tel. (011) 313599/26744*
Spacious rooms in a centrally located hotel. Delicious curry buffet lunches and à la carte dinners. Special group rates.

**71**

### Lotus Hotel

*PO Box 90193, Mombasa*
*Tel. (011) 313207*
Quiet location near Fort Jesus.

### The Manor Hotel

*PO Box 84851, Mombasa*
*Tel. (011) 314643*
One of the top hotels in the town centre.

### Oceanic Hotel

*PO Box 90371, Mombasa*
*Tel. (011) 311191/2/3*
Mombasa's largest hotel to date. Casino, swimming pool, Chinese and Middle Eastern cuisine.

## NAIROBI

### Fairview Hotel

*Bishops Road*
*PO Box 40842, Nairobi*
*Tel. (02) 723211, fax 721320*
Set in 2ha (5 acres) of beautiful gardens in the tradition of a country hotel. TV and video. About 2km (1 mile) from city centre.

### Heron Court

*PO Box 41848, Nairobi*
*Tel. (02) 720740/1/2/3*
*Fax 721698*
Double rooms or self-catering accommodation. Quiet swimming pool, sauna and massage, two restaurants, bar, shops.

### Milimani Hotel

*African Tours & Hotels*
*PO Box 30471, Nairobi*
*Tel. (02) 336858, fax 218109*
Set in a quiet, residential suburb about 2km (1 mile) from the city centre. Restaurant, bar, swimming pool.

### New Stanley Hotel

*PO Box 30680, Nairobi*
*Tel. (02) 333233*
In the heart of town. Busy and comfortable hotel with large, air-conditioned rooms. Swimming pool, restaurant, and the famous Thorn Tree Café (see p.79).

### Nairobi Safari Club

*Inter-Continental Hotels*
*PO Box 43564, Nairobi*
*Tel. (02) 330621, fax 331201*
Luxurious, elegant and exclusive. 146 suites. Swimming pool, health club, small gym.

### Norfolk Hotel

*PO Box 40064, Nairobi*
*Tel. (02) 335422, fax 336742*
Charming, distinctive hotel, and Nairobi's oldest. Set in lovely gardens, complete with aviary, swimming pool, health club, beauty salon, gourmet restaurant and the Delamere Terrace bar and restaurant (see p.78). Choice of rooms, suites and luxury cottages.

## Terminal Hotel

*PO Box 43229, Nairobi*
*Tel. (02) 228817*
This is a recommended budget hotel, with basic facilities, well located in the centre of town.

## Windsor Golf & Country Club

*Windsor Hotels International*
*PO Box 74957, Nairobi*
*Tel. (02) 219784/217497*
*Fax (02) 217498*
As its name would suggest, this hotel is set in parklands with beautiful views of the surrounding countryside – and only 15 minutes from downtown Nairobi. Elegant cottages, studio suites and double rooms. Golf club, health club, sports facilities, restaurants.

## LAKE NAIVASHA

## Lake Naivasha Hotel

*Block Hotels*
*PO Box 47557, Nairobi*
*Tel. (02) 335807, fax 340541*
Splendid hotel, the only one on Lake Naivasha.

## Safariland Lodge

*PO Box 72, Naivasha*
*Tel. (0311) 20241*
Tennis courts, golf course, horseback riding. Accommodation in cottages.

## LAKE NAKURU

## Lake Nakuru Lodge

*PO Box 561, Nakuru*
*Tel. (037) 85446*
*Booking Office: PO Box 70559, Nairobi*
*Tel. (02) 224998/226778*
*Fax (02)230962*
Comfortable rooms and four-poster-bed suites in an old stone farmhouse; swimming pool, bar, lounge, restaurant, entertainment.

## Sarova Lion Hill Lodge

*Sarova Hotels*
*PO Box 30680, Nairobi*
*Tel. (02) 333248, fax 211472*
Good views of the lake, delicious food, well-stocked curio shop. Accommodation in 60 chalets. Good for wildlife and birdwatching.

## NORTH COAST

## Bamburi Beach Hotel

*Malindi Road*
*PO Box 83966, Mombasa*
*Tel. (011) 485611*
Favourite British retreat.

## Inter-Continental Mombasa

*PO Box 83492, Mombasa*
*Tel. (011) 485811*
Luxurious self-contained resort; health club and all the trimmings. **73**

### Mombasa Beach Hotel ▐▐▐

*PO Box 90414, Mombasa*
*Tel. (011) 471860, fax 472970*
*Bookings: African Tours & Hotels*
*PO Box 30471, Nairobi*
*Tel. (02) 336858, fax 218109*
Air-conditioned, five restaurants, bars, tennis, mini-golf, large pool, watersports and long water slide.

### Neptune Beach Hotel ▐▐

*PO Box 83125, Mombasa*
*Tel. (011) 485701-3*
*Fax (011) 485705*
Set in lush tropical gardens, à la carte restaurant, pool, boutiques. Bus service daily. Wide variety of entertainments. 80 rooms.

### Nyali Beach Hotels ▐▐▐

*Block Hotels*
*PO Box 47557, Nairobi*
*Tel. (02) 335807, fax 340541*
Ideal location on fine palm beach. One of Kenya's oldest beach hotels. Two pools, outdoor jacuzzi, watersports, squash, disco.

## SAIWA SWAMP NATIONAL PARK

### Sirikwa Safaris Guest House ▐▐

*c/o Mrs Barnley's House*
*Box 332, Kitale*
Charming retreat. Accommodation in guest house (book in advance) or in furnished, spacious tents on the lawns taking meals in the guest house. Camping facilities on the grounds for independent travellers.

## SAMBURU NATIONAL RESERVE

### Larsen's Tented Camp ▐▐▐

*Block Hotels*
*Central Reservations Office*
*PO Box 47557, Nairobi*
*Tel. (02) 335807, fax 340541*
Luxurious facilities, outstanding comfort, excellent cuisine – and great for wildlife spotting.

### Samburu Lodge ▐▐▐

*Block Hotels*
*Central Reservations Office*
*PO Box 47557, Nairobi*
*Tel. (02) 335807*
*Fax 340541*
Cottages or permanent tented accommodation. Peaceful, comfortable. Swimming pool.

### Samburu Serena Lodge ▐▐▐

*Serena Lodges and Hotels*
*PO Box 48690, Nairobi*
*Tel. (02) 710511, fax 718103*
Popular lodge along the river with terrace bar, swimming pool, barbecues, leopard baiting platform. 54 rooms, 8 luxury suites.

## SHIMBA HILLS

### Shimba Hills Lodge    ▯▯
*Block Hotels*
*Central Reservations Office*
*PO Box 47557, Nairobi*
*Tel. (02) 335807, fax 340541*
This, the only tree-hotel on the coast overlooks a pretty waterhole. Good service, very comfortable, dining hall, central facilities. Sundowners and bush safaris.

## TAITA HILLS GAME SANCTUARY

### Salt Lick Lodge and    ▯▯▯
### Taita Hills Lodge
*c/o Hilton Lodges*
*PO Box 30624, Nairobi*
*Tel. (02) 332564, fax 339462*
Salt Lick is slightly more expensive, but also more unusual in design, with circular rooms standing high above the ground. Both overlook waterholes.

## TSAVO NATIONAL PARK

### Kilaguni Lodge    ▯▯▯
*African Tours & Hotels*
*PO Box 30471, Nairobi*
*Tel. (02) 336858*
*Fax 218109*
Long-established, five-star lodge with waterhole.

### Tsavo Safari Camp    ▯▯▯
*PO Box 30139, Nairobi*
*Tel. (02) 227136/338888/9*
Permanent tented accommodation. Private bathrooms with hot and cold water. Swimming pool.

### Ngulia Lodge    ▯▯▯
*African Tours & Hotels*
*PO Box 30471, Nairobi*
*Tel. (02) 336858, fax 218109*
Mecca for birdwatchers. Swim. pool, views, small airstrip nearby. Waterhole and leopard baiting.

### Voi Safari Lodge    ▯▯▯
*African Tours & Hotels*
*PO Box 30471, Nairobi*
*Tel. (02) 336858, fax 218109*
Most popular lodge in Tsavo, built into the side of the hill. Swim. pool, waterhole, photographic hide.

## WATAMU

### Hemmingways    ▯▯▯
*PO Box 267, Watamu*
*Tel. (122) 32624, fax 32256*
Upmarket establishment. Watersports, deep sea fishing.

### Turtle Bay Beach Hotel    ▯▯
*PO Box 10, Watamu*
*Tel. (122) 32622/32080*
*Fax 32268*
Ideal base for the attractions of Watamu Marine National Park.

# Recommended Restaurants

Wining and dining in Kenya won't cost the earth, even at the finer restaurants. You can eat well at most establishments at far less than European or American prices. Most restaurants fall into the moderate range: a two or three-course meal for two including drinks will cost between 500 and 1,000Ksh. Outside Nairobi and the coast your choice of eating places is slim. The hotels and lodges are your best bet for reliable fare. (For details on average prices, refer to PLANNING YOUR BUDGET, p.133.)

## CENTRAL HIGHLANDS

### Aberdare Country Club
*Lonrho Hotels Kenya Ltd*
*PO Box 58581, Nairobi*
*Tel. (02) 216940, fax 216796*
The buffet lunch attracts crowds of passing tourists; lovely lawns with views of Mount Kenya and the Aberdares; gourmet food in the evenings.

### Mount Kenya Safari Club
*Lonrho Hotels Kenya Ltd*
*PO Box 58581, Nairobi*
*Tel. (02) 216940, fax 216796*
The buffet lunch is a bonanza not to be missed! Spectacular grounds with a superb view over Mount Kenya.

## KERICHO

### Bell Inn
*Old Naivasha Road, Kericho*
A good place to stop for a quick refreshment.

### Kericho Tea Hotel
*Box 75, Kericho*
*Tel. (0361) 30004/5*
Wonderful setting among Kenya's tea plantations. Lunch, afternoon tea, dinner.

## MOMBASA

### Bella Vista Restaurant
*Moi Avenue,*
*(near information bureau)*
*Mombasa*
*Tel. (011) 225848*
Grills, seafood and curries.

### Dragon Pearl
*Moi Avenue, Mombasa*
*Tel. (011) 21585*
Open daily for Chinese cuisine prepared by Chinese chef.

### Geetanjali's
*Msanifu Kombo Street, Mombasa*
*Tel. (011) 26260*
Serves inexpensive, all-you-can-eat Asian meals. Good vegetarian food.

## Hong Kong Restaurant

*Moi Avenue, Mombasa*
Tel. (011) 226707
Authentic Chinese dishes in a delightful Chinese atmosphere.

## Mombasa Blue Room

*Haile Selassie Avenue*
*Mombasa*
Tel. 224021
Quick, informal meals are the speciality of the house.

## New Chetna Restaurant

*Haile Selassie Avenue*
*Mombasa*
One of the best places to go in Mombasa for a tasty vegetarian curry.

## Splendid View Café

*Maungano Road, Mombasa*
Tel. (011) 312048
Still the best for barbecue; meat, seafood and vegetable curries. There's a wide choice of seafood and grills.

# NAIROBI

## African Heritage Café

*Kenprop Building,*
*Banda Street, Nairobi*
Tel. (02) 333157/335707
Your chance to try African dishes. Lunch and dinner at very reasonable prices.

## Alan Bobbe's Bistro

*Caltex House*
*Koinage Street, Nairobi*
Tel. (02) 336952, 226026
For delightful French cuisine.

## Carnivore

*Langata Road*
*Nairobi*
Tel. (02) 501709/501775
Very popular restaurant, serving game meat, chicken, beef and lamb roasted over a charcoal pit.

## Foresta Magentica

*Corner House, Mama Ngina Street*
*Nairobi*
Tel. (02) 728009/23662/3
Impressive fresh dishes. In the evening, it is intimate and exclusive with cocktails and wines. A la carte menu. Live band.

## The Golden Candle Restaurant

*Ralphe Bunche Road, Nairobi*
Tel. (02) 720480
Continental cuisine with some Indian, seafood. Well-stocked bar and a pleasant atmosphere.

## The Horseman

*Karen/Langat Road, Nairobi*
Tel. (02) 882033/882782
Food at this popular establishment ranges from Chinese or Italian to English.

**77**

## Ibis Grill

*Norfolk Hotel*
*Harry Thuku Road, Nairobi*
*Tel. (02) 335422*
Smart, informal dining in the most beautiful surroundings. Open for lunch and dinner Monday to Friday and dinner only on Saturdays and Sundays.

## Jardin de Paris

*French Cultural Centre*
*Loita at Monrovia Street*
*Tel. (02) 336435*
Good food, including some interesting French cuisine. Occasional live music.

## Jax Restaurant

*1st Floor Old Mutual Building*
*(opposite IPS building)*
*Kimathi Street, Nairobi*
*Tel. (02) 23427*
Relaxing atmosphere, clean and simple food, prompt service and inexpensive prices make up this establishment's popularity.

## Lord Delamere Terrace

*Norfolk Hotel*
*Harry Thuku Road, Nairobi*
*Tel. (02) 335422*
Good lunches and light meals at this popular bar and meeting place; the cuisine doesn't stray too far from good average international fare.

## Marino's

*NHC House*
*Aga Khan Walk, Nairobi*
*Tel. (02) 336210/337230*
Italian restaurant serving good traditional dishes and good wine.

## Red Bull

*Silopark House*
*Mama Ngina Street, Nairobi*
*Tel. (02) 335717*
A cosy, crowded eating place, where they serve large portions of hearty and nourishing dishes.

## Sagret Equatorial Hotel

*Milimani Road, Nairobi*
*Tel. (02) 720933*
A *nyama choma* restaurant serving roast meats Kenya style.

## Safeer

*Hotel Ambassadeur*
*Tom Mboya Street, Nairobi*
*Tel. (02) 336803*
For quite delicious South Indian cooking with a menu of spicy Mughal dishes.

## Shield and Spear

*Utamaduni Crafts Centre*
*Langata South Road, Nairobi*
*Tel. (02) 891798*
Gazpacho and other Continental fare at this garden restaurant in the Utamaduni Crafts Centre. Lunch and dinner.

## Tamarind

*National Bank Building*
*Harambee Avenue, Nairobi*
*Tel. (02) 338959/220473*
Seafood is a speciality at this well-known restaurant.

## Thorn Tree Café

*New Stanley Hotel*
*Kimathi Street, Nairobi*
*Tel. (02) 333233*
Rather mediocre food, but great atmosphere in this famous travellers' watering hole.

## Three Bells

*Utali House*
*Uhuru Highway, Nairobi*
*Tel. (02) 220628*
Inexpensive Indian restaurant, tucked away in a business complex: curries at lunch and dinner.

## Trattoria

*Town House, Wabera/*
*Kaunda Street, Nairobi*
Open 8.30am to 12 midnight. Ristorante, pizzeria, posticceria, cafeteria, gelateria.

# NORTH COAST

## Galana Steak House

*Sunline Tennis Centre*
*(north coast of Mombasa)*
As the name indicates, steaks are the speciality of the house. Quality beef and salads at quite resonable prices.

## Imani Dhow Restaurant

*Severin Sea Lodge*
*Tel. (02) 485001/5*
Great seafood dishes.

## La Pagoda

*Travellers Beach Hotel*
*Tel. (011) 485121-6*
Open from noon till midnight. An exclusive menu and an executive chef who has 'mastered the craft of making the best pizza in town' have helped to make the Pagoda's reputation.

## Mamba Village

*Nyali, opposite the*
*Nyali Golf Club*
*Tel. (011) 472709/472341*
Specializes in local crocodile meat; seafood and steak also served. African buffet every Sunday.

## Maxim's Cellar

*Mombasa Beach Hotel*
*Tel. (011) 471861*
Exquisite French cuisine and grill room.

## Tamarind

*(north coast of Mombasa)*
*Tel. (011) 471747*
Seafood restaurant that serves good, fresh dishes.

**79**

## SOUTH COAST

### Maharani
*Diani/Ukunda*
*Tel. (127) 2439*
Specializes in tandoori cuisine. Lovely setting. Call for transport arrangements.

### Tradewinds Hotel
*Diani/Ukunda*
*Tel. (127) 2016*
Great outdoor African barbecue every Saturday night.

### Vulcano Restaurant da Lina
*Diani/Ukunda*
*Tel. (127) 2004*
Italian restaurant specializing in seafood and cuisine from Emilia Romagno.

### Wasini Island Restaurant
*Wasini Island*
*Tel. (127) 2331*
Five-course seafood lunch: fresh, whole crab steamed in ginger, barbecue fish with Swahili sauce.

## LAMU ISLAND

### Bush Gardens
*On the waterfront*
Known for its seafood and kebabs, but stop in for breakfast and try the delicious mango pancakes

### Hapa Hapa
*On the waterfront*
Great seafood: try grilled jumbo prawns or shark and barracuda kebabs.

### Petley's Inn
*On the waterfront, centre of town*
Best known for its popular rooftop bar; also serves good food.

### Yogurt Inn
*Harambee Avenue,*
*southern end of town*
Also called the Coral Reef, it's set in a shady garden and serves excellent curries, coconut rice and a daily special; good vegetarian food.

## MALINDI

### Blue Marlin
*North side of town*
*Tel. (0123) 20440*
Excellent dining room open to the public; menu varies nightly.

### Driftwood Beach Club
*South side of town*
*Tel. (0123) 20155*
Popular for good seafood.

### Trattoria
*North side of town,*
*across from the Blue Marlin*
*Tel. (0123) 20710*
Good pizzas and pasta, cold beer.

## LAKE VICTORIA

The broad, clean streets and white buildings of **Kisumu** are a pleasant surprise for the travel-weary. In this languid, lakeside town you can go about your business without any hassle from the beggars and souvenir sellers you encounter elsewhere. Either it's just too hot to bother, or this inland port, which has long served as a crossroads for African, Asian and European traders takes foreigners for granted.

In 1901 the railway line at last reached Port Florence, as the town was then called, completing a trade link with Uganda across the lake. Great heat, humidity, as well as outbreaks of sleeping sickness, malaria and blackwater fever made it the least desirable posting in the British Empire. But by the

*A fishing boat sails slowly past sacred ibis on the shores of Lake Victoria.*

start of World War II it had become a major East African transportation hub and administrative centre. Kenya's third-largest town fell into decline with the disbanding of the East African Community in 1977 and the drop in lake traffic. Today it has a mixed aura of charm and decay, and even an air of optimism as light industry replaces the rusting ships and empty warehouses along the shore.

 Highly recommended is a visit to the **Kisumu Museum**, a short walk or ride east of town. An incredible specimen of taxidermy stands, on its forelegs, in the main exhibition hall: a frantic wildebeest with an attacking lioness clinging to its back. Less dramatic but equally interesting are the collections of musical instruments displayed here. (You will also see toys and other traditional artefacts of West Kenyan ethnic groups.) The museum grounds contain a Luo homestead, an unexciting aquarium, a turtle pond, crocodile pit and a snake house brighter than the one in Nairobi.

In the town itself, Kisumu's **market** is delightful, the largest in western Kenya and a good place for a browse and a bargain. But the real attraction here is **Lake Victoria**, the second-largest freshwater lake in the world. The main roads are inland from the water's edge, so you can't really stroll along the shore, and, sadly, swimming is absolutely out of the question, as bilharzia, a nasty parasite, is present in the water. The best way to enjoy the lake is to take a boat trip or ferry from the dock to one of the small islands.

Alternatively, you can enjoy spectacular sunsets over the lake from your balcony at the **Sunset Hotel**, in an affluent suburb south of the town centre, where all rooms look out across the water. If you are staying in town, head out to Hippo Point, just past the hotel, for a similar view. You can also visit the fishing village of **Dungas** a bit further on, where the morning's catch of Nile perch and tilapia is unloaded, filleted and sold at the local fishmarket.

# KERICHO

Before or after your trip to Maasai Mara, particularly if you've spent a long time on the hot, dry and dusty road, you may find yourself, for the first time in your life, crying out for rain. There's one place that guarantees satisfaction – Kericho with its famous tea plantations about 250km (155 miles) north-west of Nairobi. Almost every day, at 3pm, dark clouds gather and burst into refreshing showers.

You can enjoy this spectacle from the comfort of your armchair at the **Tea Hotel**, where the unmistakable Englishness of the immaculate green lawns and flower gardens is a welcome change from the arid, red savannah. Built in 1952 as a clubhouse for the Brooke Bond tea company, to stay at the hotel is to take a delightful step back in time. The place is a swan song of the colonial era, and the rooms have their original Fifties-style furnishings. Even the old crank telephones remain! Afternoon tea is served on the patio or in the sitting room with its chintz curtains and kitschy furniture.

The tea plantations are well worth a visit. There are miles of lush green bushes tightly packed in a shoulder-high carpet dotted with the heads of tea-pickers plucking the buds and topmost young leaves and tossing them into wicker baskets on their backs. With advance arrangements, you can also visit the local tea factories on estates near the town for an explanation of the cutting, fermenting and drying stages that go into tea processing.

Kenya's tea industry prospered in the 1920s when experts decided Kericho's soil was perfect for producing the best quality tea from Ceylonese and Indian plants. You suddenly realize how the British Empire functioned as a gigantic holding company, enabling the transfer of whole industries from one continent to another. Today the Kericho plantations cover approximately 15,000ha (37,000 acres), and the tea industry as a whole lies just behind tourism as Kenya's main foreign income earner. **83**

## MAASAI MARA NATIONAL RESERVE

If your trip to Kenya allows you time to visit only one game park, make it this one. **Maasai Mara**, geographically an extension of Tanzania's renowned Serengeti National Park, gives you the best chance of seeing all the major wild animals in a superb rolling landscape of gentle hills and majestic acacia woodland.

This is one of the few places left in Africa where you can see great animal herds roaming the plains in the vast numbers that early explorers once witnessed. Between the end of July and November, over one and a half million **wildebeest**, accompanied by half again as many zebras and gazelles, migrate from the Serengeti Plains to fresh pasture in the grasslands of the Mara, creating one of nature's grandest spectacles. Moving in groups of up to 20,000 at a time, they thunder across the plateau, hesitating one second at the Mara River until the pressure of their numbers forces the leaders to plunge into the swirling waters. Many perish before reaching the opposite bank, drowning in the rushing river or victims of the waiting crocodiles.

You'll see lots of **lions**: the Mara has the largest population of them in Kenya, and you'll have the best chance of spotting a leopard in the wild in these parts. The waters of

*The Maasai adorn themselves with colourful cloaks and beaded jewellery.*

84

the Tana and Mara rivers are abundant with hippo; there are large herds of elephant and buffalo, and a rhino sanctuary.

The Mara is Maasai country; Mara, in fact, is a Maasai word meaning 'spotted' or 'mottled', a reference to the acacia trees dotting the vast plain. The 1,670sq km (645sq mile) area is a national game reserve, and Maasai herdsmen are permitted to reside with their cattle on parts of the land.

Off-road driving is still allowed in this reserve. While it

---

### The Maasai

The Maasai are Kenya's most famous tribe. This proud, nomadic people once ruled, through sheer ferocity, the fertile grasslands of the Rift Valley, and the plains from Lake Turkana to Kilimanjaro. For centuries, they have herded cattle in search of water and fresh pasture, clinging to ancient traditions and resisting the encroachment of modern life.

Several related families live together in low, circular huts constructed by the women out of mud mixed with cow dung. Their diet consists of milk, maize and blood extracted from their cattle, which they rarely use for meat. The size of a Maasai's herd is a symbol of his wealth. The Maasai believe that God gave them all the cows in the world; the other animals belong to God and must not be harmed; only eland and buffalo, the 'wild cattle', can occasionally be hunted for food.

The Maasai are polygamous, and they still practise the circumcision and initiation rites that take a male from boyhood to warrior status. Despite conflict with the authorities, these proud, young *morani* who carry clubs, swords and spears still see the killing of a lion as a measure of manhood.

The Maasai do not take kindly to being photographed; ask their permission first. But it will not be too difficult to get a shot of these tall, striking people adorned with colourful beads, jewellery and bright red cloaks tied at the shoulder. Many have conceded to tourism and will happily pose for a fee.

gives you the opportunity to seek out the more elusive game across the plain or among the thickets, you must be careful not to drive too close or disturb the animals and their prey. It is advisable to have a four-wheel-drive vehicle and enrol the help of a guide who knows the area when driving off the marked tracks.

The remoteness of Maasai Mara adds to its adventure. Flying is the most convenient way to get there, and there are several small airstrips serving the lodges with daily flights. Though the 260km (160-mile) drive across the Rift Valley from Nairobi is scenic in parts, the roads into the park from Narok or Kericho can be atrocious after heavy rain. Be prepared to push. Accommodation is plentiful, with lodges, permanent tented camps and a good number of campsites.

Mount Kilimanjaro lies in Tanzania, close to the Kenyan border. It can be seen from a distance in Tsavo.

# The South-East

## AMBOSELI NATIONAL PARK

Although the wildlife is abundant and easily accessible, the most important reason for recommending this particular park is that the giraffes, elephants, cheetahs an other animals and you are likely to see there become an unforgettable spectacle against the backdrop of **Mount Kilimanjaro**. Except

## Kilimanjaro

'As wide as all the world,' wrote Hemingway in his famous short story, 'great, high and unbelievably white in the sun.' The legendary Kilimanjaro is Africa's highest mountain, at 5,895m (19,342ft). This massive, extinct volcano has three marvellous peaks. The highest is the great snow-covered table known as Kibo, but called Uhuru (freedom) since Tanzania gained independence. The western peak, Shira, is only 4,005m (13,140ft) and the jagged eastern peak is Mawenzi, 5,150m (16,897ft) high but much tougher to climb than Kibo.

Legend has it that the son of King Solomon and the Queen of Sheba, King Menelik of Abyssinia, also made it to the top. In heroic battles he conquered all of East Africa and then, as death approached, he climbed Kibo. He disappeared into the crater with his slaves, who carried all his jewels and treasures, including King Solomon's ring. Find that ring and you'll inherit Solomon's wisdom and Menelik's courage. Failing that, take a good look at one of the great wonders of the world, all the more splendid for standing there alone and unchallenged.

for the very beginnings of its northern foothills, Kilimanjaro is entirely inside Tanzania, but the awe-inspiring view of it from anywhere in Amboseli makes it an undeniable part of Kenya's landscape, too.

This relatively small park, which can be covered in a day, receives heavy tourist traffic: short-term visitors dashing down from Nairobi and safari vans trekking through to near-by Tsavo. On the positive side, hordes of roving tourists make a poacher's job difficult, and as a result Amboseli is Kenya's foremost elephant park, boasting some of the country's finest mature specimens. A herd of 40 or more elephants in the mellow evening sun setting over Kilimanjaro is a truly impressive sight.

Amboseli's environment is a precarious one. Its swamps **87** provided the Maasai with a natural watering hole until the land was declared a national park in 1973. By then the combination of overgrazing and increased tourism had turned vast areas into near desert, and a sudden rise in the water table brought toxic salts to the surface, killing many trees. Extensive damage has also been caused by too much off-road driving. Lake Amboseli dried up to little more than a puddle for many years. Then, unseasonal torrents of rain in January 1993 flooded the park. It's unlikely that this popular park will ever get the breathing space it needs to fully recover. Amboseli serves as a reminder of the fragility of a seemingly rugged landscape.

## TSAVO NATIONAL PARK

**Tsavo** is the largest national park in Kenya. Its territory of 20,800sq km (8,030sq miles) has been split into two separately controlled parks, divided by the Nairobi–Mombasa highway.

Enormous **elephant** herds once roamed the plains of Tsavo, along with the largest population of black rhino in Africa, numbering in the high thousands. But in the past two decades, more than three quarters of the elephants and nearly all of the rhino have been wiped out by a lethal combination of successive droughts and ruthless poaching.

The Kenyan government's anti-poaching forces, strongly focused on Tsavo, have been largely successful in stopping the slaughter. However, the whole northern sector of Tsavo East has been closed to the public as park rangers continue to wage war against the armed poachers.

The surviving elephant families – sadly devoid of their elders – tend to congregate near the park lodges and roads for safety, making them easy to see and photograph. The rhino sanctuary in Tsavo West shelters most of the remaining rhino, though you may still be able to spot one in the wild in the Rhino Valley between the park's two lodges. The rest of the Big Five are well represented, and these, along with the wealth of other wildlife from the ubiquitous Marabou stork to the rare lesser kudu, account for Tsavo's popularity as a game-viewing mecca.

**Tsavo West** has the most spectacular landscape, an undulating plain peppered with green hills and rounded buttes which are a legacy from the area's recent geological past. The nearby Chyulu Hills were created by volcanic action less than 500 years ago, and the Shetani Lava Flow on their southern edge is only 200 to 300 years old. There are trails leading across the lava rock to the top of the hill and into the Shetani Cave – bring a torch and walk with care. You can also scramble up the brittle, black slope to the rim of the Chaimu Crater, formed by another lava fountain. Always be alert for wild animals when exploring any of Tsavo's volcanic ruins.

The park's star attraction is the lush oasis of **Mzima Springs**. Rain falling in the Chyulu Hills is purified as it soaks through porous volcanic ash, and runs underground for 50km (31 miles) to resurface in two crystal-clear pools at Mzima. It is then piped to Mombasa to provide most of the city's drinking water. Walk along the cool, luxuriant path through the palm trees and reeds lining the banks of the pools, home to crocodiles and hippos, and stop at the viewing tank submerged in the upper pool for a fish-eye's view of barbels and mud suckers. Crowds of vervet and Sykes monkeys hang about in the fig trees.

Three rivers – the Galana, the Athi and the Tsavo, – flow through the park, attracting large concentrations of game. But the denser growth of vegetation after a period of rain can make it very difficult to see the animals. Rain also brings out that scourge of Tsavo, the tsetse fly. This variety does not carry sleeping sickness, like those in the Congo, but they have a nasty sting and will sometimes swarm in the open windows and roofs of safari vans when driving through a thicket. A blast of insect spray

**89**

is the best way to rid your vehicle of these invaders (who are also said to be attracted to the colour blue!).

The park has two lodges: **Kilaguni**, Kenya's oldest park lodge, and **Ngulia**, which offers some fine views across the plain. The latter park is on a bird migration corridor and ornithologists from all over the world gather here to study the migration patterns of the many species. Both Ngulia and Kilaguni have waterholes which attract a variety of wildlife.

**Tsavo East**, the larger of the two parks, is flatter, drier and less visited except for **Voi Safari Lodge**, built into the side of a hill with a fantastic vista across the sweeping plain. It, too, has a floodlit waterhole complete with a photography hide alongside.

At the time of writing, tourists were discouraged from visiting Lugard's Falls and the Yatta Plateau for security reasons. Do check out the current situation with rangers at the gate before travelling there. It used to be possible to climb **90** Mudanda Rock, but as it has

become a popular viewpoint for lions as well as tourists, this is no longer advisable. A tamer sight is the popular, man-made **Aruba Dam** which attracts abundant game in the dry season.

# Mombasa and the Coast

## THE ISLAND CITY

Whether it's your first port of call on a package tour, or a stop-over en route to a seaside retreat after the rigours of safari, arriving in **Mombasa** seldom fails to infuse your senses with a touch of the exotic. Perhaps it's the heat, or the smell of the sea; or perhaps it's just the contrast of brilliantly patterned *kangas* set against stark, white mosques and black *buibuis*, between pristine Hindu

*The tranquil terrace of the Mombasa Beach Hotel overlooks the Indian Ocean.*

temples and the teeming chaos of the market.

This island city is the crossroads of Africa and Asia, and Kenya's oldest town. Its status as a port and trading centre is no less important now that tea and tourism have replaced gold and ivory as chief commodities. Beneath its sultry veil, Mombasa thrives as it has always done, exuding an air of vitality in slow motion.

Mombasa's origins may well stretch as far back as 500 BC, when Phoenician sailors put in at a coastal port that would correspond to Mombasa Island. The Greeks noted its trading potential in the 1st century AD, and later dhows, carried by the north-east monsoon from the Persian Gulf across the Indian Ocean, sailed along East Africa's coastal reef and found a navigable opening at Mombasa. It became a magnet for Arabs, Persians, Turks, Indians, Portuguese and the British, all of whom left their mark on the

town. Mombasa's history is a pattern of fighting off a foreign foe, then absorbing him and fighting off the next one.

In the 7th century, enterprising merchants from Persia and Arabia began to settle in the 'Land of the Zanj' (Land of Black People), bringing with them the Islamic faith. Over the next 300 years, the intermingling of races and religions produced the Afro-Arab language and culture of Swahili.

Mombasa basked in wealth and power until the end of the 15th century, when the Portuguese arrived to plunder the coast. It took nearly a hundred years of repeated assaults before the island stronghold fell, but that century of siege destroyed mediaeval Mombasa. The town you see today is essentially 19th century, except for the remains of Fort Jesus, built by the Portuguese for their garrison in 1593. They in turn were driven out in 1730, and a period of unrest followed in which Mombasa was ruled by the feuding Omani families who had aided the rebellion against the Portuguese. In the late 19th century, as a British protectorate, the town flourished once again.

Sightseeing in Mombasa can easily be covered in a day. This is best done as early in the morning as possible, before your enthusiasm sinks into the torpor of the midday heat. The one monument you won't miss coming into or out of town is the **double arch**

*The Swaminarayan Temple is one of Mombasa's most colourful Hindu temples.*

92

across Moi Avenue formed by four huge, white, sheet-metal tusks, erected in 1955 to commemorate the visit of Princess Margaret. The tourist information office sits just beyond the 'elephant' tusks.

**Fort Jesus**, on the edge of the old town, is a good place to begin your tour. Strategically placed at the southern entrance to Mombasa harbour, it stands on a coral ridge and has ramparts several metres thick. Inside you can make your way along the parapet walk, step up on the firing positions and imagine what it must have been like to defend this redoubt against marauding infidels – Muslims or Christians or 'pagans' according to who held it, since both the Portuguese and the Arabs made it their stronghold right up to 1895, when the British took over and turned it into a prison.

The fort has retained the same basic shape throughout its tumultuous 400-year history. The grounds include a barracks, chapel, water cistern and well, guard rooms, gunpowder storeroom as well as an Omani house filled with artefacts from the Arab period.

During the Arab conquest in 1698, the powder magazine was the scene of an act of mad heroism: a Portuguese officer told the Arabs the storeroom held the garrison's gold treasure, led some Arab soldiers to collect it and blew them and himself to smithereens.

The cannons in the courtyard are English naval guns brought there in 1837. The fort also has a small museum with a collection of artefacts from up and down the coast.

The **old town**, just north of Fort Jesus, is the most fascinating part of Mombasa. Along the main thoroughfare of Ndia Kuu Road you can see some of the city's finest Arab buildings with intricately carved doors and delicate wooden balconies. The narrow streets contain many of Mombasa's 49 mosques, the oldest of which is the **Mandhry mosque** on Bachawy Road, built in 1570.

Lovely Hindu temples can also be found throughout the city. Among the most striking are the Swaminarayan Temple on Haile Selassie Avenue, the Jain Temple off Digo Road, and the Lord Shiva Temple on the edge of the old town.

Gone are the days when tourists were welcomed aboard to join the haggling at the old **dhow harbour**. The policemen at the entrance will let you pass for a few shillings, but you'll see handfuls, not hundreds, of these ancient craft. You can watch the loading or unloading of the last of the dhows that still ply between Mombasa and the Gulf, their large lateen sails now supplemented by a motor, but photographs are strictly forbidden – so keep your camera well out of sight.

You can wisely ignore the glut of ambitious curio shops near the Fort Jesus car-park, which are largely overpriced. A more authentic atmosphere for browsing can be found at the **Municipal Market**, still known by its colonial name, Mackinnon's Market. The adjacent Biashara Street is an excellent place to browse and shop for bright-coloured *kangas* and fabrics. Moreover, if you haven't seen quite enough wooden elephants and other carved creatures yet, head out to the **Akamba Woodcarving Cooperative**, on the airport road, where some 3,500 craftsmen from this eastern province work here and you can wander through the workshops between piles of ebony lions and teak giraffes and chat with them about their trade.

*The sea is the sculptor of the lovely coral rock formations on Wasini Island.*

## THE SOUTH COAST

The Likoni Ferry links Mombasa to the south coast. Here you'll find that idyllic palm-fringed beach with soft, white sand of your dreams. Protected by a coral reef, the water off shore is warm and clear; surprisingly, the beaches here are quieter than most of the north coast's resort areas.

The best of the beaches is **Diani**, whose major landmark, near the Trade Winds Hotel, is a 500-year-old baobab tree

**95**

measuring 21m (71ft) in circumference, protected by presidential decree. Once you have seen the baobab, there is blissfully little to do but watch the sun rise and set, an often spectacular event.

There are plenty of watersports on offer all along the coast. Highly recommended is  an excursion to **Wasini Island** and **Kisite Marine Park**. You will be collected from your hotel early in the morning for the hour's drive south to Shimoni, where a converted dhow takes you past coral islands

to Kisite. The reef here offers

some of the best snorkelling on the coast, but you can also gasp at the amazing corals and tropical fish by looking through glass-bottom viewers from a small boat.

Following a gigantic seafood lunch at the Wasini Island Restaurant, you are entirely free to relax in the gardens or explore the island's early 19th-century Muslim village. On its edge are the stunning coral gardens. These surreal, honeycombed sculptures, spread over nearly 1ha (some $2\frac{1}{2}$ acres), were chiselled out by the fluctuating tides over the past 200

*he idyllic white sands of Diani beach at the Trade Winds Hotel (left), and the residents of Mamba village (right).*

years. They remain, naturally, a work in progress.

If you want to give your suntan a rest, you can go inland to the little game reserve at **Shimba Hills**. The pleasant, wooded plateau rises to 450m (1,475ft), giving a refreshing change from the oppressive heat of the coast. Go early in the morning for the best chance to see the splendid sable antelopes with their scimitar-shaped horns, rare in Kenya. The males have magnificent coats of reddish-black, while the females are a lovely chestnut-brown colour. There are no lions, so it is safe for the antelopes and you to walk on the higher slopes – but look out for the odd python!

Another popular excursion, though further inland, is the privately owned game sanctuary at **Taita Hills**.

## THE NORTH COAST

The north coast is where Mombasa's Asian, European and African elite have their homes, palatial residences shrouded in hibiscus and bougainvillea. The area abounds in luxury hotels, for the most part well run, which will live up to your expectations of the 'good life'.

There are several attractions to divert you from the sun and sea. **Mamba Village** is the largest crocodile farm in Africa. You can walk along a shady pathway to observe some of its 10,000 reptiles basking in a series of breeding pools reclaimed from an old limestone quarry. Five o'clock is feeding time, when you can watch the **97** jump as high as 2m (…ft) out of the water for their dinner. There are also lovely botanical gardens, an aquarium with live corals, camel and horseback rides and a restaurant serving, it goes without saying, crocodile steaks.

The Swiss agronomist Réné Haller was awarded a UN environmental protection prize for his success in converting the wasteland of a stone quarry into the **Bamburi Nature Trail**. This small forest now harbours serval cats, monitor lizards, owls and other wildlife, including a pair of hippos in the central lake. Nearby is the **Bombolulu Workshop** for the disabled, where you can buy original jewellery, bags and other crafts at very reasonable prices.

On a bush tour into the countryside, you'll see coconut palms, cashew nut and baobab trees, and sweeping sisal plantations (a cactus-like plant used for weaving rope and baskets). The local Giriama live in traditional villages of earth and thatch houses, tending small plots of pineapple, tobacco and other crops.

## North to Malindi

There are two sets of Arab ruins as you head north to Malindi. The first is at **Jumba La Mtwana** (Home of the Slave Master), a 14th-century Swahili town whose ruined coral houses and mosques stretch down to the sea.

More substantial is the ancient town of **Gedi**, founded in the late 13th or early 14th cen-

*Feeding the tropical fish at the Malindi Marine Park.*

**98**

tury. The ruins here are extensive and well preserved; you can seek out the old mosques with their deep wells along eery trails through the jungle, or pick your way among the walls of the palace, houses and pillar tombs. Rooms such as the 'House of the Scissors' and 'House of the Venetian Bead' indicate where Gedi's most interesting finds were made, many of which can be seen in the small museum.

Just outside Gedi you'll find the enchanting **Watamu Marine National Park**. Like its neighbour, **Malindi Marine National Park**, it is a protected area of white, coral sand beaches and clear, deep-blue lagoons where it is forbidden to both fish or collect coral and seashells.

A visit to these wonderful marine parks is a must, especially if you are staying in Malindi, where the sea is often brown with the mud of the Sabaki River. From any of the hotels at Watamu or Malindi you can arrange a trip in a glass-bottom boat out to the coral reefs, where you can view these marvels of nature by skin-diving and snorkelling. Be sure to bring along a couple of loaves of bread, and you'll have swarms of brilliantly coloured tropical fish eating out of your hand.

## Malindi

If you've had a hard year and just want to bask for a week or two in the sun, then **Malindi** may be the place for you. Visitors are well catered for in this old Swahili town, which now relies solely on tourism for its prosperity. There is some excellent fishing and a pleasant market to browse through for souvenirs. However, it's usually too hot to move around, so you don't have to feel guilty about relaxing by the pool until you fly home.

There was a time when Malindi was more lively. With an eye to the main chance, the Sheikh of Malindi welcomed Vasco da Gama on that 1498 journey, giving him provisions for his voyage to India. His hospitality paid off with some golden years of trade with **99**

Portugal during the 16th century, until the rival state of Mombasa was conquered and the Portuguese transferred the sheikh there (see p.12). Malindi then sank back into the torpor you'll encounter today.

There's a monument to that brief moment of glory, out along the cliffs on the promontory, at the southern end of the Malindi harbour. The brilliant white **Vasco da Gama pillar**, engraved with Portugal's coat of arms, was erected by the explorer in gratitude to the sheikh for his warm reception. It has survived the ravages of the Turks, Arabs and British and is one of the very few authentic Portuguese relics left on the coast.

A more exotic adventure can be found 8km (5 miles) inland at the newly opened, private game sanctuary at **Lake Chem Chem**. Here you can go on a camel safari through the hills and valleys around the lake to see the area's bird and animal life, ending up with a sunset barbecue and entertainment by native dancers – a great day out!

## Lamu

For an idea of what Malindi – or Mombasa for that matter – really looked like when the Arabs ruled the coast, make the trip to the island of Lamu, a delightful backwater of Swahili culture basking peacefully off Kenya's northern shore. Its origins date back to the 2nd century and along with Manda and Pate it was one of the most prosperous commercial centres of the archipelago until its decline in the late 1800s. Unlike its neighbours, Lamu survived, remaining isolated from modern technology and the western world until shipping and the great wave of tourism brought a resurgence to its economy in the 1960s.

It is best reached by small aircraft on one of the regular, inexpensive flights from Malindi or Mombasa, as the overland route is very rough and often flooded. You'll be welcomed at the airstrip on Manda Island by an eager gang of locals ready to carry your bags to the ferry for the short crossing to Lamu.

Your first few hours in Lamu may prove something of a cultural shock. There are no cars here; the main mode of transport is donkeys – and they and their droppings are everywhere. Open sewers run alongside the narrow streets and refuse is often dumped into the sea. But you soon forget the unsanitary sights and smells as you fall into the languid rhythm of this town.

The traditional Islamic community has made few concessions to the modern world. Women, especially, should be dressed in a conservative manner to avoid causing offence, though you'll feel pretty conspicuous in shorts when everyone else is swathed in black from head to toe.

Here's a perfect chance to do as the locals do and wrap a colourful *kikoi* around your waist. And be extra sensitive about photographs here; always ask before you point your camera at someone. Having said that, you'll find that the people of Lamu are some of the friendliest you'll meet anywhere. Nobody works too hard; they

*E*xplore the wildlife of the north coast on a camel safari at Lake Chem Chem.

fish a little, tend their shops, and have plenty of time to chat to strangers.

Lamu's stone houses are undoubtedly the best legacy of Swahili architecture. These plain, thick, coral walls often conceal elaborate interior ornamentation of carved plasterwork and wall niches. You can see a fine example, restored to portray the early way of life, at the **House Museum**.

The most beautiful feature of Lamu's houses is their carved wooden doors. Some date **101** back to the 18th century, but even the most modern retain the style, forms and craftsmanship of centuries-old traditions. There are excellent specimens on display at the **Lamu Museum**. One of the finest small museums in Kenya, it offers good explanations of Lamu's architecture and insights into the traditions of this complex culture. The pride of the museum is two magnificent *siwas* (ceremonial horns), one of carved ivory 2m (6½ft) long and the other, slightly shorter, of brass.

You can eat seafood for a song at the small restaurants along the waterfront, but only two places on the island sell alcohol (by way of compensation, you'll find delicious fruit milkshakes everywhere). The first is **Petley's Inn**, a landmark meeting place for locals and travellers alike; head up to the rooftop bar. The second is the **Peponi Hotel**, 3km (2 miles) down the road at Shela. This is Lamu's swimming beach, easily reached by motorized dhow if you don't want to walk.

There are plenty of local boatmen to take you fishing or sailing on a dhow around the other islands. But the best way to spend your days in Lamu is to wander aimlessly through its back streets, or simply sit on a rooftop or in the main square by the old fort, watching this timeless world go by.

*W*all niches called vidaka adorn Lamu's old Swahili houses, while the rooftops provide a view of the sea.

# What to Do

## Sports

### Fishing

Kenya offers a wide range of opportunities for sports and outdoor recreation year-round due to its excellent climate. Though hunting has been banned since 1977, deep-sea or big-game **fishing** has taken over as Kenya's lure for the outdoorsperson. It's ranked among the best in the world.

All along the coast, you'll find fishing clubs and boat-charter services, many of which have desks at the major hotels. You can hire anything from a little speedboat with an outboard motor to a luxury yacht or sportfishing cruiser equipped with heavy gear in the 50lb and 80lb classes. All boats are licensed and come with an expert crew, rods, reels, bait and all the harness equipment necessary to haul in the big ones. When negotiating the price, be sure first to determine the number of passengers allowed and whether you get to keep any fish caught, which you can sell, if you wish, to defray the costs of boat hire.

The eight-month fishing season runs from early August until the end of March, though some boats do continue to fish through the rainy season. Try to get out to sea (or the lake) in the morning and you can expect to grapple with barracuda, kingfish, yellow-fin tuna, sailfish and tiger and hammerhead sharks. The mightiest opponent you are likely to encounter is the marlin, which can weigh up to 300kg (660lb).

Although fishing is forbidden in the marine parks, there are specified places along the coast where spin casting from small boats, and fishing from shore are allowed.

Inland, you can enjoy fine fishing for rainbow or brown trout in the streams around Mount Kenya, the Aberdares, the Kericho district and up at Mount Elgon. Lake Naivasha is famous for its black bass and tilapia. Fishing camps are located in most regions. Most equipment can be hired and you need a licence.

One of the greatest thrills is fishing for the big Nile perch; the largest caught to date, from Rusinga Island, weighed in at 92kg (203lb). Lake Victoria has surpassed Lake Turkana in the far north as the best place for Nile perch. Even with dwindling fish stocks, Turkana still provides a remote fishing adventure, and the chance for a furious fight with a tiger fish.

## Watersports

Watersports of all types are prolific throughout Kenya. You will find the coastal waters delightfully warm for swimming, with none of the health risks or crocodiles of the inland rivers and lakes. The sharks stay outside the reef.

If you've never gone **snorkelling** before, there couldn't be a better place to give it a try than Kenya's amazing coral reefs. There are **glass-bottom boats** for hire at hotels and on the beach which will take you out to these shallow reefs, and many of them have snorkelling

*A* successful catch of Nile perch at the Rusinga Island Fishing Club on Lake Victoria.

gear on board. Wear rubber-soled shoes to protect your feet from the razor-sharp coral. **Scuba diving** equipment can also be hired, and many hotels offer diving tuition.

Some beach resorts offer **waterskiing**, and **windsurfing** is also on the rise. You can, in **105** theory, waterski on some of the inland lakes, but the possibility of contracting bilharzia makes it a risky business; stick to the coast.

**Sailing** is a great way to enjoy the inland waterways, the best spots being Lake Naivasha, Nairobi Dam and Lake Victoria. If you're visiting Lamu Island, a dhow trip around the nearby islands is a timeless thrill. **Canoeing** is also a growing sport, and river trips can be arranged at many lodges and hotel resorts.

## The Great Outdoors

Kenya's spectacular moutains and scenic hills make **hiking** a great lure. Some of the most accessible regions for walking include Mount Kenya, the Aberdare Mountains, the Chyulu Hills, Hell's Gate, and Mounts Susua and Longonot and the Menengai Crater in the Rift Valley. Ngong Hills, south-west of Nairobi, popular with ramblers, have recently been the scene of muggings and are no longer considered safe. Further afield, the Cherangani Hills and Mt Elgon are both considered superb walking country. Before setting off, pick up a good guidebook and detailed map specific to the region you plan to visit.

Experienced and fearless **mountain climbers** can attempt an ascent to the higher peaks of Mount Kenya. Climbs are organized by the Nairobi-based Mountain Club of Kenya and begin at the Naro Moru River Lodge, which hires out porters and equipment. A reasonably fit novice can climb the lower peak, Lenana, in a couple of days.

## Leisure Activities

**Golf** remains a popular sport, with golf hotels and country clubs catering to the golfer's every whim. There are no less than ten 18-hole golf courses within a 30km (19-mile) radius of Nairobi. The scenic Karen and the Muthaiga Country Clubs (par 72 and 71 respectively) are the best known. The Royal Nairobi Club, with its delightfully old-fashioned clubhouse and museum, and

*Island Camp offers waterskiing on Lake Boringo; watersports such as windsurfing, snorkelling, scuba diving and sailing abound along the Kenya coast.*

Limuru Country Club, possibly the most difficult course, are also popular.

Apart from Nairobi, there are three other main golfing circuits: the Central Highlands, the west and the coast. The mountain circuit offers cooler weather and gently undulating courses with impressive views. The west is more seasonal, with afternoon rains; at Eldoret's 15-hole course you play across the river at least three times – watch out for the water. Bring along your own equipment. Some of the clubs have quaint rules of penalty and compensation if your ball is given a helpful kick or is eaten by a passing animal. In elephant footprints, for example, bunker rules usually apply.

**Tennis** and other racket sports are on offer at many of the larger hotels and sports

...os. **Gymnasiums** are gradually being fitted in at some of the international hotels.

**Riding**, an imperial legacy, is most popular in the Highlands. A good place to enquire about hiring horses is the Karen shopping centre outside Nairobi. Pony trekking through the Rift Valley or elsewhere can often be arranged through your lodge or hotel.

**Horse-racing** has been a popular sport in Kenya since the turn of the century, though the only racetrack to hold regular meetings is at Ngong, outside Nairobi. The season runs from September to July, when meetings are held most Sunday afternoons.

# Photography

Kenya's dramatic landscapes and awesome wildlife make it a photographer's heaven, and few people come without a camera. Specialized photo safaris are organized in the same way as the old hunting safaris, some of them on a grand scale with luxury tents and fine cuisine. However, you'll still take some great photographs on the group game runs. The safari vans and land cruisers have pop-up roofs to give you unimpeded standing shots, and you will often find the animals so close that your telephoto lens will be a hindrance.

One of the problems with the group runs is that when one vehicle has found a pride of lions basking in the sun, other vehicles will rush to the spot and encircle the poor animals, limiting photographic alternatives. It is a good idea, if the terrain allows it, to pull back from the lions once you have found them, and shoot telephoto at a distance in such a way that other groups won't notice your find.

You won't need a lot of specialized equipment. A single-reflex lens (SLR) 35mm camera with an automatic focus is ideal. A telephoto lens is useful for wildlife shots, otherwise, when you see your prints, you'll often find the animals have shrunk to the size of a pea. But many people have had good results with a simple

35mm compact camera with a built-in zoom facility. Most animals are shy and won't wait around to give you a perfect pose; the quickest photographer often gets the best shot.

People are another matter. Be sensitive to the various cultures you will come across; some tribes fear that a photo will capture their soul. Always ask permission before taking someone's photo, particularly Muslim women and tribes like the Maasai and Samburu. On the other hand, while some people object to undignified invasions of their privacy, others will demand payment for posing. This is usually negotiable, but if they ask too much there will always be another opportunity down the road, where you may even find tribesmen flagging down your vehicle to do a dance for you – not exactly *cinéma vérité* but colourful all the same – for an appropriate fee.

When you do photograph people, keep in mind that dark skin against a bright background is a difficult exposure to get right: bracket several frames if your camera allows it. Early morning and late afternoon offer the best light for most photography. Keep your film and cameras out of direct sunlight, away from extreme heat, and well protected against dust and damage from the rough roads. Take extra batteries and twice as much film as you think you'll need. Film stocks aren't reliable in the bush, and even in town you can't be sure of its quality.

# Camping

'Roughing it' in Kenya's great outdoors ranges from pitching your own tent in a clearing among the trees to luxury camping safaris where your every need, from chilled wine to clean latrines, is provided. If you want to go it alone at one of the many campsites across the country, you can hire four-wheel-drive vehicles fully kitted out with camping gear.

There are campsites at all of the major game parks and several private campgrounds with varying facilities. Don't **109** expect too much in the way of showers, fresh water, toilets or other creature comforts.

Dangers from wild animals are relatively small, given that most will shy away from humans unless provoked. There are snakes everywhere, but they'll slither away before you see them. More threatening are the mosquitoes – bring plenty of insect repellent – and the scavenging monkeys and baboons. Lock your food in the car, never in your tent. Most campsites have an armed *askari* to watch over things at night and deter any curious creatures, including humans. Theft is a problem at the more popular campsites and along the coast, so never leave any valuables unattended.

## Shopping

The big challenge in shopping for souvenirs of your stay in Kenya is sorting out the true, genuine artwork from mass-produced junk. The first rule of thumb is to avoid any shop **110** with a sign that offers 'curios'.

These may well be hand-carved as advertised, but on an assembly line, without the careful craftsmanship of the real thing. The better shops offer handcrafted woodcarvings of finer quality and design, such as those made by the Akamba.

Two good places in Nairobi to find authentic, quality African crafts are Utamaduni, off

A decorative drum made by the Giriama tribe of Kenya's north coast.

Langata Road, which donates a percentage to wildlife conservation and African Heritage, with a huge showroom on the Mombasa Highway. You can find cheaper goods at the city market, but you'll have to bargain hard. Prices are usually doubled for foreigners, so start your haggling at half the suggested price. Crafts co-operatives representing rural artisans have retail shops in the towns, and you can often visit textile, bead and woodcarving workshops on the outskirts.

Soapstone animals, candlesticks, plates, etc are also popular, but the larger items are heavy, and soapstone can easily chip or crack if not packed with great care. *Kiondos*, the traditional, woven sisal handbags, come in many colours and make good gifts.

In Mombasa shop for antiques: Arab brasswork, trays and Zanzibar chests. You'll find good buys, but nothing will be inexpensive. The coast is also a good place to buy colourful fabrics – *kikois* for men, *kangas* and *kitangas* for women – which can be worn

*Colourful printed textiles brighten a crafts shop at Utamaduni in Nairobi.*

as beach wraps or used for bedspreads and tablecloths.

Animal skins bought without government permits – and you won't get one – are strictly illegal, as are game trophies and ivory products. Coral and sea shells will probably have been plundered from one of the protected marine parks, so that their purchase should be discouraged.

**111**

# ntertainment

The big show is Kenya itself, but if you occasionally have an urge for discotheques or nightclubs, Nairobi, Mombasa and the coast hotels can satisfy your needs. You'll often be entertained by bands performing American and European pop music. Acrobat floor-shows have become a popular diversion at many of the discos and hotels. Nairobi, Mombasa and Malindi all have casinos for the gambling crowd.

Traditional African music can be difficult to find. Native dancing is often performed at the lodges and hotels, but it sometimes bears the same relationship to the real thing as the curios in souvenir shops do to authentic African art.

A more genuine display of African dancing is available at the Bomas of Kenya, near Nairobi National Park, where you can see Samburu war dances, Kamba acrobatics, a Giriama wedding dance and an expurgated version of the Kikuyu circumcision ceremony – still carried on by men though suppressed by women, feminism being a growing movement in Kenya.

The free publication *What's On* will give you a rundown of current exhibitions, plays and cultural events in the capital. Nairobi's Gallery Watatu and the Paa ya Paa gallery display contemporary African art.

*A*crobats put on an impressive show in the lounge at Lake Nakuru Lodge.

# Eating Out

Wining can be very easily dealt with: drink the **beer**. Kenya's local brews – Tusker, Premium and White Cap – are excellent and inexpensive, served cool or warm according to your preference. In hotels and restaurants all imported wines and spirits are expensive. Imported red wines suffer in the heat, and white wines are refrigerated out of all recognition. The more daring *bons vivants* can try Kenya's own fruit wines made from papaya and pineapple, or the very potent palm wine. The Lake Naivasha vineyards produce a very drinkable white. After dinner, try the coffee liqueur, Kenya Gold.

Eating out in Kenya owes much, probably too much, to the colonial past. Most hotels and lodges offer a faithful reproduction of English cuisine,

but the 'meat and two veg' varies greatly in quality and preparation, more often than not bland and overdone.

Inland, the ubiquitous **Nile perch** is often the alternative choice. However, quantities are enormous and cheese and desserts are an honourable supplement to the meal, especially with the delicious, ripe pineapples and mangoes. Also, on the game reserves, you will be glad of the full English breakfasts served after an appetite-building dawn game run.

The great, truly great exception to this is the **seafood** served on the coast: large lobsters, superb shrimp and prawns, all astoundingly cheap compared with European or American prices – and excellent kingfish

*K*enya's beers are a perfect accompaniment to the scenery at the Aberdare Country Club.

and swordfish. If you order them simply grilled, with at most a butter sauce, you will have Kenya's best meals.

**Vegetarians** get short shrift at the lodges, but fare better in the cities and on the coast, where there are many fine Indian and Chinese restaurants. After a long, arduous safari, a pizza never looked so good and you'll find the best ones on the north coast in Malindi.

**African food** can best be sampled at the African barbecues put on weekly by many hotels. The meat is accompanied by clay pots filled with sweet potatoes, arrowroot, cassava and other root vegetables. Instead of potatoes, try a side dish of *ugali*, a kind of polenta made from maize.

The rural staple, *sukuma wiki* (which literally translates 'getting through the week') makes for an interesting variation on spinach. *Irio*, a Kikuyu mixture of mashed chick peas, corn, pumpkin and potatoes, is another dish to try, as is *kuku wakupaka*, a spiced chicken recipe from Lamu. Also look out for restaurants serving *nyama choma* (roast meat) which often consists of goat, chicken or beef.

The buffet service, favoured by most hotels for at least one of their daily meals, gives you as generous portions as you could wish. In Kenya, to eat well without spending a fortune, go for the buffet spreads and seafood.

*F*resh crab is a highlight of the seafood lunch at the Wasini Island Restaurant.

114

# BLUEPRINT
## for a
## Perfect Trip

# An A–Z Summary of Practical Information

A

## ACCOMMODATION

(See also CAMPING, p.118 and the list of RECOMMENDED HOTELS AND RESTAURANT, P.66)

Kenya's tourist hotels are classified as Town Hotels, Vacation Hotels, Lodges and Tented Camps. In addition, there is self-catering accommodation. Most towns have rudimentary 'boarding and lodgings', as they are called, which offer little more than a bed, well water and minimal security; these are not recommended for tourists.

**Hotels**. Kenya's hotels vary enormously in price and facilities, and the one-to-five star rating given by the Ministry of Tourism is not an accurate basis of comparison. It's better to enquire at a local travel agent, or book through one of the larger hotel chains. Kenya's luxury hotels offer extremely high standards of service and are comparable to the best hotels anywhere in the world. First- and second-class hotels vary widely in service and facilities, but are generally comfortable with private bath and European-type food. Hotel prices are often discounted during the low season and there is usually a reduction for children under 12. Book early!

**Lodges**. Accommodation is limited in the national parks and reserves, so lodges must be booked well in advance, especially during high season. Food and facilities are generally of good to high standards.

**Permanent Tented Camps**. These permanently sited canvas tents are pitched on a concrete base or raised wooden platform. Many offer a surprising degree of luxury, with flush toilets, hot and cold running water and electricity.

**Self-catering**. Self-help *bandas* are available in many game parks. These African-style thatched huts offer cooking facilities, which

**116**

vary considerably from a propane gas stove to a campfire; you will need to bring your own bedding, food and drink. These are popular with Kenyans during high season and public holidays, so book ahead. In towns, some of the larger hotels offer apartments or boarding houses for extended stays. Self-catering villas, apartments or cottages are becoming more widely available, especially on the coast. Check with a travel agent, or try contacting Kenya Villas, PO Box 57046, Westminster House, Kenyatta Ave, Nairobi, tel. (2) 29161 who act as agents for many holiday homeowners.

## AIRPORTS

Kenya is served by two of the largest, most modern and efficient international airports in Africa. The **Jomo Kenyatta International Airport** is half-an-hour's drive from Nairobi's city centre, where most of the better hotels are located. Mombasa's **Moi International Airport** on the Kenya coast is closer to the town centre, but most of the tourist hotels are at various distances from the town. Porters will take heavy bags to customs for you, free of charge; other porters will assist you to bus stops and taxi stands for modest tips.

Most tourist hotels have their own minibuses at the airports to transport guests, while airlines provide transport to terminals in the city centres. Kenya Airways buses leave on the hour to a central terminal, stopping at main hotels on the way and every hotel within Nairobi. A public bus serves both the Jomo Kenyatta and Moi airports. Numerous taxis are on hand.

Kenya Airways buses leave the city-centre terminals at Nationwide House, Koinange Street, Nairobi and Electricity House, Nkrumah Road, Mombasa, on the hour.

**Departure**. There is an **airport tax** for departing passengers which must be paid in **foreign currency** (see also PLANNING YOUR BUDGET, p.133). Duty-free purchases can only be made in foreign currency. Check your baggage allowance with your airline and do not exceed it, as overweight charges can run into 500Ksh per kilo!

**Flight information**. Jomo Kenyatta Airport, Nairobi: tel. 822111 or 822206. Moi Airport, Mombasa: tel. 433211.

**Internal air travel**. Domestic flights are a convenient and affordable means of travel. Kenya Airways have regular flights to Mombasa and Malindi. Frequent scheduled and charter flights operate from Nairobi's Wilson Airport and from Mombasa and Malindi to the main towns and game parks. There is an airport tax of 50Ksh for internal flights.

## B

### BARGAINING

Bargaining is very much a part of life in East Africa, and it is particularly useful in markets and curio shops. Some seasoned shoppers advise that you start your bargaining at half the suggested price. If prices are marked, there is probably little room for negotiation.

### BABYSITTERS (*msaidizi wa kutazama mtoto*)

Most hotels will arrange babysitting services for their guests. Rates vary widely depending on the location of the hotel or lodge, and on the number of children, but are never excessive.

## C

### CAMPING

Some people would say camping is the only way to experience the real Kenya. Wherever you want to camp, you are certain to be surrounded by magnificent scenery, and in some places, by a wide range of wildlife. You can book sites on the spot or at the town hall.

Camping has become a thriving 'extra' for Kenya's tour operators, and the better-off visitor can experience the thrill of Kenya's vast skies and the endless bush at a comfortably fitted campsite. But for the enterprising visitor (and resident alike), camping in Kenya's wild bushlands can be an inexpensive and unforgettable experience.

**Site**. Find a site well before sunset, for in tropical Africa it can be pitch dark half-an-hour after the sun starts to go down. Choose level ground with short grass and plenty of shade, but beware of the type of tree you camp under: thorn trees are good for shade and have no climbing leopards and snakes, but you'll usually find a thick carpet of thorns underneath them. Make sure the rear windows face the prevailing wind. Do not set camp on, or too near, a sandy expanse of a dry river-bed – a tropical rainstorm miles away can send unbridled water gushing down towards you. Avoid camping right across or too near a game trail –you could find an animal stumbling into your guy ropes. In addition, there is always the danger of a fire going wild. Learn to build 'safe' fires and keep the flames under control at all times.

**Camping equipment**. If you intend spending the whole holiday under canvas, bring as much equipment as your weight allowance will permit. The main items include: tent (with a sewn-in groundsheet and mosquito-netted windows); camp beds, sleeping bags; folding chairs and table; local pots and pans (Kenyan lightweight ones are excellent for direct fire use); plastic airtight containers; axe and machete; *karai* – a metal bowl useful for heating water, for washing, or covering the fire when it rains; a two-burner gas stove with spare gas; torch (flashlight); plates, mugs, spoons, etc; folding spade; wooden bread board; gas lamps; insulated boxes; personal equipment; binoculars; plenty of drinking water; food (plan with care depending on which part of the country you are heading towards); safari clothes.

## CAR HIRE (See also DRIVING, p.123)

To hire a car you must be over 23 and under 70 years of age and possess a valid driver's licence from your country of residence, or an international driver's permit. The driver must have held the licence for a minimum period of two years at the time of hiring a vehicle.

All the major international car-hire firms are represented in Kenya, and numerous local firms offer competitive rates. Prices are higher than in Europe and North America. A deposit and daily collision damage insurance are compulsory. Safety rather than price should be your first consideration in choosing a car hire firm: a breakdown in a remote area or game park is more than an inconvenience – it can pose **119** a real danger. Confirm in writing that if the car breaks down the car hire company will replace it with another vehicle. *Always* check the oil, water, tyres, and engine; determine the grade of petrol required and ensure you have at least one good spare and the essential tools. If possible, hire the car a day in advance of setting out on the road in order to drive around town and check the condition of the vehicle.

Although 4-wheel-drive vehicles are not essential, they are preferred in game parks and reserves.

## CLIMATE

Since Kenya is on the equator, the climate remains pretty stable throughout the year. Days are sunny and hot, but nights can be cool. The weather is warm and dry from mid-December to mid-March, and the long rains fall between late March and June. July and August are a second, shorter high season. September to October are the best times to visit, as the weather is good prior to the short rains that begin in late October through to mid-December. Water temperature remains constant all year – from 23°C (73°F) to 26°C (79°F).

| Nairobi | J | F | M | A | M | J | J | A | S | O | N | D |
|---|---|---|---|---|---|---|---|---|---|---|---|---|
| °C max | 26 | 27 | 27 | 26 | 24 | 23 | 23 | 23 | 26 | 26 | 25 | 25 |
| °C min. | 13 | 13 | 14 | 15 | 15 | 13 | 12 | 12 | 13 | 14 | 14 | 14 |
| °F max. | 79 | 81 | 81 | 79 | 75 | 73 | 73 | 73 | 79 | 79 | 77 | 77 |
| °F min. | 55 | 55 | 57 | 59 | 59 | 55 | 54 | 54 | 55 | 57 | 57 | 57 |
| Rainfall (in) | 2 | 3 | 5 | 8 | 6 | 2 | 1 | 1 | 1 | 2 | 4 | 3 |
| (mm) | 50 | 75 | 127 | 200 | 150 | 50 | 25 | 25 | 25 | 50 | 100 | 75 |
| **Mombasa** | J | F | M | A | M | J | J | A | S | O | N | D |
| °C max | 32 | 32 | 32 | 31 | 29 | 29 | 28 | 28 | 29 | 30 | 31 | 31 |
| °C min. | 23 | 24 | 24 | 24 | 22 | 22 | 21 | 21 | 21 | 22 | 23 | 23 |
| °F max. | 90 | 90 | 90 | 88 | 84 | 84 | 82 | 82 | 84 | 86 | 88 | 88 |
| °F min. | 73 | 75 | 75 | 75 | 72 | 72 | 70 | 70 | 70 | 72 | 73 | 73 |
| Rainfall (in) | 1 | 1 | 3 | 8 | 13 | 5 | 4 | 3 | 3 | 3 | 4 | 2 |
| (mm) | 25 | 25 | 75 | 200 | 330 | 127 | 100 | 75 | 75 | 75 | 100 | 50 |

## CLOTHING

Lightweight, cotton casual wear is fine on safari, and a hat and sun-glasses are recommended for protection against the strong sun. Bright colours are best avoided, as they can attract insects and make you too conspicuous in the bush. Evenings in Nairobi are cool, and can be quite chilly in the Highlands. Warm clothing is necessary after sunset. At lower altitudes, a long-sleeved shirt and long trousers are a deterrent to mosquitoes. Trainers are the most versatile footwear – you may want to bring hiking boots if you plan to do a lot of walking in the bush, and waterproof shoes during the rainy seasons.

Jacket and tie are needed only in the classiest restaurants. Nylon and other synthetic materials prove very hot for the coast; cotton is much more suitable. Nudity and topless sunbathing on the beaches or in any public place are forbidden in Kenya.

## CRIME

Some areas in Nairobi and Mombasa are best avoided after dark; take a taxi. Avoid going into poorly lit areas or buildings in the towns, cutting through city parks at night, or strolling alone on empty highways, lanes or on the beaches at night.

Do not carry large sums of cash or traveller's cheques with you. Deposit what you do not require immediately with the manager of your hotel for safe-keeping. Lock all articles in the boot of your car, and lock the car too. Similarly, do not leave valuable personal belongings unattended on beaches and in public places. It's best to leave expensive jewellery at home. Be careful of pickpockets.

For those travelling upcountry on their own, there is the possibility of attacks by armed bandits, called *shiftas*, in certain areas. Police stations and army posts along the route will have current information on the area and will arrange guarded convoys if necessary.

## CUSTOMS AND ENTRY FORMALITIES

Australians, New Zealanders, Americans, South Africans and British passport holders of Indian, Bangladeshi or Pakistani origins need to obtain a visa. Citizens of Great Britain, Ireland and Canada don't need one. A three-month visitor's pass is issued free on arrival. All other nationals should apply for a visa from one of the embassies or consulates in their country. Make sure your passport is valid for at least six months beyond the proposed end of your stay.

The following chart shows what main duty-free items you may take into Kenya and, when returning home, into your own country.

| Into: | Cigarettes | | Cigars | | Tobacco | Spirits | | Wine |
|---|---|---|---|---|---|---|---|---|
| Kenya | 200 | and | 50 | and | 70g | 1l | or | 1l |
| Australia | 200 | or | 250 | or | 250g | 1l | or | 1l |
| Canada | 200 | and | 50 | and | 400g | 1.1l | or | 1.1l |
| Eire | 400 | or | 100 | or | 500g | 1l | or | 2l |
| New Zealand | 200 | or | 50 | or | 250g | 1.1l | or | 4.5l |
| S. Africa | 400 | and | 50 | and | 250g | 1l | and | 2l |
| UK | 200 | or | 50 | or | 250g | 1l | or | 2l |
| USA | 1,000 | and | 100 | and | * | 1l | or | 1l |
| * A reasonable quantity | | | | | | | | |

**Currency restrictions**. You can bring any amount of foreign currency into Kenya and take it out again when you leave. But import and export of Kenya currency is not permitted. You are advised to change your money or spend it before reaching the airport on departure (you're allowed to keep 200Ksh per person for drinks in the departure lounge). You may be able to change it at the airport, but the Mombasa Airport bureau de change closes at 7pm. You will need to show your last currency exchange slip.

# D

## DISABLED TRAVELLERS

Kenyans generally have a helpful attitude towards disabled travellers. Most of the larger hotels in town and on the coast have lifts. Traffic is a bigger problem; be careful crossing the busy streets. In the game parks, negotiating narrow stone paths at some of the lodges may be difficult in a wheelchair. Seek advice from a knowledgeable travel agent when choosing a lodge. Also, the rough, bumpy roads may cause discomfort even in the most luxurious safari van.

# DRIVING IN KENYA

Driving in many parts of Kenya is at best a challenge and at worst a nightmare. If you are on holiday, you may want to leave much of the driving, especially on the unpaved sandy and muddy roads, to experienced and well-trained tour drivers.

Shipping your car to Kenya is not recommended, as auto thefts have soared in recent years. If you do, you would be wise to check beforehand how long you are allowed to use it without having to pay import duty. Have it cleared by customs as soon as it arrives, or you'll have heavy storage charges to pay. To take your car into Kenya you will need: an international driving licence; car registration papers; an international insurance certificate; a nationality plate or sticker.

**Driving conditions**. Kenyan motorists drive on the left and overtake (pass) on the right. Most vehicles have the steering wheel on the right. Roads are generally narrow, so make sure you have full view of the stretch ahead before you attempt to overtake. Road conditions in many places are appalling: even the main Nairobi–Mombasa highway is full of dangerous potholes. Drive slowly on rough roads to maintain control of your vehicle. Be prepared for unexpected manoeuvres and remember that driving standards are as poor as the roads.

Dirt roads quickly turn to mud when it rains. When approaching a nasty-looking patch of mud or water, it's best to check the depth first if possible; if not, keep moving in second gear until you're clear.

**Driving in the national parks**. Speeds are strictly limited to 40kph (25mph) and sometimes less, so as not to frighten the wild animals. For the same reason, all loud noises and brusque movements should be avoided, both when driving and while taking photographs.

## Fluid measures

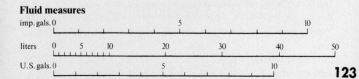

**Distances**. Here are some approximate road distances in kilometres (miles) between major centres:

| | |
|---|---|
| Nairobi–Eldoret | 310 (190) |
| Mombasa–Eldoret | 800 (495) |
| Nairobi–Kisumu | 350 (215) |
| Mombasa–Kisumu | 845 (525) |
| Nairobi–Malindi | 615 (380) |
| Mombasa–Malindi | 120 (75) |
| Nairobi–Marsabit | 560 (350) |
| Mombasa–Marsabit | 1,110 (690) |
| Nairobi–Mombasa | 490 (305) |
| Mombasa–Moyale | 1,380 (855) |
| Nairobi–Nanyuki | 200 (125) |
| Mombasa–Nakuru | 650 (405) |
| Nairobi–Nyeri | 160 (100) |

## To convert kilometres to miles

**Traffic police**. Make sure your hire car has the proper insurance and PSV (passenger service vehicle) licence stickers in case you are pulled over. For minor traffic offences, the police impose fines on the spot. You will have to appear in court and pay the fine in cash.

**Breakdowns**. Before setting out for long-distance driving, get in touch with the Automobile Association of Kenya: its headquarters are in Nairobi. The AA will advise on the road conditions ahead, and on how you can obtain help in case of emergency. When travelling off the main routes, consider taking jerry cans of petrol and water. If you do have a breakdown, spare parts and proper tools may be scarce. Agree on the price with local mechanics before any work begins.

**AA Telephones**. Nairobi: (02) 720382; Mombasa: (011) 26778; **124** Eldoret: (0321) 22700; Kisumu: (035) 41361; Nakuru: (037) 44811

## ELECTRIC CURRENT

Major towns and cities are supplied with 240 volts, 50 cycles AC.
Some lodges have independent power generators which vary in volt-
age. Tourist hotels and lodges generally provide an adaptor for 220
and 110 volts. The plug in use throughout Kenya is of the three-pin
13-amp type.

## EMBASSIES, CONSULATES, HIGH COMMISSIONS

Kenya maintains diplomatic relations with more than 80 countries.
Many countries also have consuls in Mombasa.

**Australia**: High Commission: Riverside Drive, PO Box 39341,
Nairobi; tel. 445034/9.

**Canada**: High Commission: Comcraft House, Haile Selassie
Avenue, 6th Floor, PO Box 30481, Nairobi; tel. 214804.

**Ireland**: Embassy: Macndeleo House, 4th Floor, Monrovia Street,
PO Box 30659, Nairobi; tel. 226771/2/3/4.

**New Zealand**: Contact the Kenyan local authorities or the UK High
Commission.

**S. Africa**: South African Trade Mission, Temple Bar House,
corner of Baker Avenue and Angwa Street, Harare; tel. 707901

**UK**: High Commission: Bruce House, Standard Street, 3rd Floor,
PO Box 30465, Nairobi; tel. 335944/60.

**USA**: Embassy: Embassy Building, Moi Avenue, PO Box 30137,
Nairobi; tel. 334141/50.

## EMERGENCY TELEPHONE NUMBERS

If your hotel desk clerk isn't available to help, here are some emergency numbers:

Police, Fire, Ambulance anywhere in Kenya: **999**

Police Headquarters, Nairobi area: **(02) 335124**

Police Headquarters, Mombasa: **(011) 25501**

St John's Ambulance, Nairobi: **(02) 24066**

## GETTING TO KENYA

### FROM GREAT BRITAIN

**By air**. Kenya Airways and British Airways have daily, direct flights from London (Heathrow) to Nairobi (some flights are direct to Mombasa), stopping at different places en route according to the day of travel. Passengers from Ireland and the provinces must connect at London. There are flights linking Nairobi to Mombasa and other airports in Kenya. The fares available are first class, economy class, excursion and APEX. The price of an APEX ticket (low compared with other fares) varies according to the season – June to September and December to January are considered 'high' seasons.

**Package tours**. A comprehensive range of tours is available, from full board in a top class hotel including safaris, to budget accommodation with optional excursions. Safaris are often organized for groups with special interests. For the independent traveller, it is often possible to purchase flight-only tickets on these charter flights.

**By sea**. Mediterranean Shipping Lines have passenger berths on their cargo ship which sails once a month from Felixstowe. The 28-day voyage goes through the Mediterranean and the Suez Canal and stops at Mogadishu, Dar-es-Salaam, Tanga and Mombasa. Strand Cruise Centre in London (tel. 071-836 6363) is the main agent in Britain for the line.

**By road**. From Europe to Kenya: via North and West Africa. You can join overland package holiday groups driving from London to Nairobi.

### FROM NORTH AMERICA

**By air**. Nairobi is serviced by direct flights from New York City on Tuesdays, Thursdays and Fridays. Connections can be made daily from many American and Canadian cities. Those travelling between New York, Houston or Toronto and Nairobi have the most flights and departure times from which to choose.

Three fares at present available to Kenya are economy, first class, and the 14- to 45-day excursion. The excursion fare is least expensive and can be booked at any time. It permits two stopovers in each direction if the trip is made via Europe. If travel takes place on a weekend, a surcharge must be paid. Children two to 11 years of age fly for 50% of the adult excursion rate.

**Charter flights and package tours**. A variety of Group Inclusive Tours (GIT), usually of three weeks' duration, combine visits to cities like Capetown, Cairo and Casablanca with wildlife tours of Kenya. Several programmes include Brazil as the first stopover point. From there, travel is due east to South Africa and then north to Victoria Falls, Kenya, and the Sudan. Included in the cost of the tour are round-trip air transport transfers, accommodation at de luxe hotels and lodges, all or most meals, tips, and the services of a guide. A 15-day OTC (One-Stop Inclusive Tour Charter) has been designed for travellers who want to visit only Kenya and spend nine days on safari. Previous restrictions on travellers arriving from the Republic of South Africa no longer apply.

## GUIDES and INTERPRETERS

Trained tour guides and interpreters have been graduating from the Kenya Utalii (Tourism) College (the only such centre in Black Africa) since 1974, and there are many qualified guides. Your hotel desk or the tourist information bureau should be able to recommend one. Be wary of those who approach you on the street.

L

## LANGUAGE (See also SOME USEFUL EXPRESSIONS, p.141)

Swahili, the *lingua franca* of East Africa, was originally written in Arabic characters. When British missionaries introduced the Latin alphabet, they adopted as phonetic a transliteration as possible, so that Swahili is rather easy to pronounce. More than 40 tribal languages are spoken in Kenya. Most people, however, speak English remarkably well, and so English, whatever accent you have, will be understood, except well off the beaten track, where you'll need Swahili. The Berlitz phrase book SWAHILI FOR TRAVELLERS will help you get by in just about any situation you're likely to meet.

## LAUNDRY and DRY-CLEANING
(*dobi mfua nguo; dobi wa nguo za sufu*)
Hotel laundry is generally done well and is not too expensive. If you are in central Nairobi, you may want to try one of the many fast-service dry-cleaners. Ask at the reception desk for the one nearest your hotel, as the in-house charges may be rather high. There are no self-service launderettes in Kenya.

| | |
|---|---|
| I want these clothes… | **Nataka nguo hizi…** |
| cleaned/ironed/ | **zisafishwe/zipigwe pasi/** |
| pressed/washed | **zipigwe pasi/zioshwe** |
| I need them… | **Nazitaka…** |
| today/tonight/tomorrow | **leo/usiku/kesho** |

## MEDICAL CARE

**Vaccinations**. Check with your doctor or travel clinic well in advance, as some injections need to be taken several weeks apart. In general, your polio and tetanus boosters should be up to date and you will need vaccinations against typhoid and hepatitus A. Yellow fever and cholera inoculations are advisable, but obligatory only if you enter from an infected area. However, if an outbreak of yellow fever occurs, you may be made to have one before you leave the country.

**Health Precautions**. (See also WATER, p.141.) You can safely swim in the sea, but avoid swimming, bathing in or drinking from lakes (especially Lake Victoria), rivers or open natural reservoirs because of the risk of bilharzia, parasites, typhoid or dysentery bacilli. All swimming pools are safe and usually well cared for.

Malaria is still a problem all over the country. Nairobi is officially malaria-free, but don't run unnecessary risks; take one of the several reliable prophylactics for two weeks before you arrive in Kenya, all the time you are in the country, and for four to six weeks after you return home. Consult your doctor as to the most appropriate type. In mosquito areas, sleep under a mosquito net (all good hotels and lodges provide them) and use an insect repellent; those containing DEET are recommended.

Visitors heading for the coast are advised to take all things in moderation at the start. There is a clinical condition known as 'heat exhaustion' which is generally brought about by an excess of eating or drinking, sunbathing or exercising, not just by temperature. Although sunstroke is rare on the coast, sunburn is very common since the sun is hotter and more direct near the equator.

AIDS is a serious problem throughout Africa. A recent report by the London School of Hygiene and Tropical Medicine claimed that 90 per cent of Nairobi prostitutes tested HIV positive. Sexually transmitted diseases are also common. Nairobi Hospital uses disposable needles and syringes, but many travellers carry a small kit of their own in case medical attention is needed in the more remote areas.

**Insurance**. If your medical insurance cannot be extended to foreign countries, you may want to take out special travel insurance to cover yourself in case of accident, illness or hospitalization.

**Doctors**. There are highly qualified doctors, surgeons and dentists in both Nairobi and Mombasa.

**Doctors' surgeries** are open from 8am to 5or 6pm or later. Lodges in remote game reserves have resident medical staff. The lodges have radio or telephone contact with the Flying Doctor Service in Nairobi. If travelling under your own steam, camping, etc, you should think of joining the Flying Doctor Service as a temporary member for a small fee. The postal address in Nairobi is PO Box 30125; tel. 501301/500508; fax 506112.

**Pharmacies**. Pharmacists in the major urban centres take turns to stay open late – until about 8 or 9pm; rosters are published daily in the newspapers. Pharmacies at the major hospitals remain open 24 hours a day. **129**

**Hospitals**. The major hospitals in the **Nairobi** area are all well equipped:

*Kenyatta National Hospital*; tel. 334800.
*Nairobi Hospital* (private); tel. 722160.
*Gertrude's Garden* (specializes in children's illnesses); tel. 763474.
*Aga Khan Hospital*; tel. 742531.
*Mater Misericordiae Hospital* (specializes in maternity and related cases); tel. 556666.

The major hospitals in the **Mombasa** area are fully equipped:
*Coast General Hopital* (the largest); tel. 312401.
*Mombasa Hospital*; tel. 312191.

## MEETING PEOPLE

By and large, Kenyans are friendly and easy-going, perhaps more so in Mombasa than elsewhere. In Nairobi, people are courteous but a little more businesslike in their manner. In the countryside people are amicable and often very interested in talking with visitors. In Nairobi, the most likely place for you to meet with African or European residents is at the New Stanley's Thorn Tree Café or the Delamere Terrace at the Norfolk (see p.79). In Mombasa, the discos and other nightclubs are frequented by Europeans and Africans alike. One of the best places in Kenya for meeting people is the island of Lamu, especially at Petley's Inn, and the restaurants along the waterfront.

## MONEY MATTERS

(See also CUSTOMS AND ENTRY FORMALITIES, P.121)

**Currency**. Kenya's unit of currency is the Shilling (slang: Bob), divided into 100 cents (c). It is abbreviated Sh(s) and written 1, 2/-, etc. There are copper coins of 5 and 10c and silver coins of 50c and KSh 1 and 5. Banknotes come in denominations of Shs 10, 20, 50, 100, 200 and 500.

**Exchange control regulations**. Visitors are particularly warned against those 'unofficial' money changers who will offer incredible deals in the street – you will be breaking the law and will usually end up with a handful of paper or forged notes. Foreign currency, including traveller's cheques, may be exchanged for cash only at a commercial bank or an authorized hotel.

**Banking hours**. Banks in Nairobi and the major towns west of Nairobi are generally open Monday to Friday from 9am until 1 or 2pm and from 9am to 11am on Saturday (sometimes only the first and last Saturday of the month). Banks in Mombasa and along the coast open and close half an hour earlier. Some of the banks at Jomo Kenyatta Airport are open round the clock every day. Foreign exchange departments of major banks in Nairobi stay open till 3 or 4pm from Monday to Friday.

**Credit Cards and Traveller's Cheques**. Most international credit cards are accepted in Kenya, though Visa is more widely accepted than Access or Mastercard. Traveller's cheques are readily recognized and accepted at most international hotels and tourist agencies.

N

## NEWSPAPERS and MAGAZINES

Kenya has three well-established English-language daily papers, the *Nation*, the *Standard* and the *Kenya Times*, and their Sunday counterparts. There is also a weekly English-language magazine and a wide range of monthlies. Many international newspapers and magazines are sold on newspaper stands and in stationers' shops in the large hotels several days later, at a price.

O

## OPENING HOURS

Opening hours vary slightly in Nairobi, the coast and upcountry towns, but in general:

**Banks**. 9 am to 2pm Monday to Friday, 9 to 11am first and last Saturdays of each month, excluding national holidays.

**Post Offices**. 8am to 1pm and 2 to 4.30 or 5pm Monday to Friday and 8am to 12 noon on Saturday in main post offices.

**Restaurants**. Breakfast is usually served between 7.30 and 9.30am, lunch from 12.30 until 2.30pm and dinner from around 7 or 7.30pm until 9 or 10pm. In the larger cities some restaurants will serve until midnight and you will be able to find cafés and pizzerias that serve meals throughout the day.

**Shops and Museums**. In the larger cities these are generally open from 8am until 5 or 6pm. Hours vary considerably in the smaller towns and rural areas.

P ▬▬▬▬▬▬▬▬▬▬▬▬▬▬▬▬▬▬▬▬▬▬▬▬▬▬

## PHOTOGRAPHY

Well-known brands of film are on sale, but prices are slightly higher than in Europe and the United States. You can't always be sure of the quality either, as film can be damaged by high temperatures, so it's better to bring plenty from home. Bring spare batteries as well. Zooms are useful and telephoto lenses essential for good wildlife photography in Kenya. A 135mm lens is sufficient for animals, perhaps a 200mm for birds. Some Nairobi and Mombasa photo shops have good selections of still or ciné cameras for sale or hire (expensive).

Your camera will require extra protection. While in the bush on dusty roads, keep both camera and lenses in polythene bags, preferably shopping bags, where they can be reached easily. Do not leave your camera in the sun or locked in your car in the heat and keep it away from sand and salt water. When you go through security checks, don't allow your camera and film to be submitted to detection devices.

It is *forbidden* to photograph the national flag, the President, state lodges, soldiers, prison officers, prisoners, prison establishments and any military or police buildings. Some of Kenya's more colourful tribespeople have become wise to tourist ways and may demand a small fee to pose for a photograph. Many people object to having their picture taken, so always ask permission first.

## PLANNING YOUR BUDGET

The following list will give you some idea of what to expect in Kenya; however, these prices are approximate and you should add a small contingency figure to allow for inflation. The Kenya shilling and exchange rate fluctuates widely, and most tour operators and hotels quote their rates in US dollars. Otherwise, prices are given here in the local currency.

**Accommodation**. Rates for double room, high season: Luxury hotels US$200–244 (full board); town hotels US$ 35–175 (bed & breakfast); beach hotels US$ 100–150 (half board); lodges US$ 148–212 (full board); permanent tented camps US$ 120–307 (full board).

**Airport departure tax**. US $20, £15 sterling (must be paid in foreign currency).

**Attractions**. Museums 50–100Ksh; historic ruins 50–100Ksh; Bomas of Kenya 300Ksh adult, 150 children; Mamba Village 700Ksh; visits to tribal villages 250–500; Ksh boat trips 500–2,000Ksh per hour.

**Babysitters**. 250–300Ksh per day plus transport.

**Camping**. In national parks and reserves 150–200Ksh per night with own tent; booking is usually done on arrival: fee 200–300Ksh.

**Car hire**. International firms, all inclusive rates. *Daihatsu Charade (4 seats)*: 3,900Ksh per day; 15,000Ksh per week. *Suzuki Sierra (small 4WD)*: 9,000Ksh per day; 30,000Ksh per week. *Isuzu Trooper (large 4WD)*: 15,000Ksh per day; 60,000Ksh per week. (These rates include unlimited mileage and insurance. Petrol: 25–30Ksh per litre.)

**Cigarettes** (per packet of 20). Local brands 22Ksh, American and British brands 35–40Ksh.

**Domestic flights** (scheduled). Nairobi–Mombasa (one way) 1,875Ksh; Nairobi–Kisumu (one way) 1,200Ksh; Nairobi–Maasai Mara 4,464Ksh (return); Nairobi–Nanyuki 3,924Ksh (return); Nairobi–Samburu 6,084Ksh (return); Mombasa–Lamu 4,464Ksh (return); Malindi–Lamu 2,988Ksh (return).

**Film**. Kodak Gold 24 exp. 100 ASA: 250–350Ksh.

**Game park entrance fees** (per day). 540Ksh adults and children (non-resident); 85Ksh adults, children usually free (residents), 80Ksh vehicles.

**Meals and drinks**. *Breakfast* from 120Ksh; *lunch* 130–200Ksh; *omelettes* 150Ksh; *sandwiches* 75–165Ksh; *grills* 150–205Ksh; *seafood* 135-600Ksh; *pizzas* 135-180Ksh; *curries* 120–350Ksh; *dinner* 300–550Ksh (moderate), 1,000Ksh (3-course meal in a good restaurant); *mineral water* 80Ksh (shops), 160Ksh (hotels); *sodas* 15–30Ksh; *fruit juices* 30Ksh; *beer* 20–45Ksh; *wine* (imported) 100–200Ksh per glass, from 480Ksh per bottle.

**Sports**. *Horse riding* 710Ksh per hour; *Golf*, green fee from 415Ksh; club hire from 300Ksh for a half day; *Fishing licence* 355Ksh; *Waterskiing* 650Ksh per quarter hour for boat and equipment; *Windsurfing* 250Ksh per half hour; *Big-Game Fishing* 6,500Ksh for a half day, 12,000Ksh for a full day (max. 4 people).

**Trains**. Nairobi–Mombasa, 1st class compartment for 2: 900Ksh per person; 2nd class: 500Ksh per person; 3rd class: 380Ksh per person.

## POLICE

Policemen and women are generally friendly and helpful to tourists and are the most reliable source of any kind of information you may require. There are various branches of the Kenya Police, but the two types you are likely to meet are the traffic and the criminal police. If they cannot help you, they will tell you where to obtain the information you need. In an emergency, dial **999**.

## POST OFFICES

Post offices are indicated by the letters PTT (Post, Telephone, Telegraph). Mail boxes are painted red. You can also buy stamps at hotels and souvenir shops selling postcards.

Send any packages or important letters to Kenya by registered mail to ensure they reach their destination. When mailing items home there are some size limitations, and parcels must be wrapped in brown paper and tied with string. Parcels must be examined for customs at the appropriate post office unit before they are wrapped.

**Main Post Offices**. The main post office for poste restante and general services is on Haile Selassie Avenue in Nairobi and on Digo Road in Mombasa.

**Post Restante (General Delivery)**. Address mail with your name, poste restante, GPO, town. In the smaller post offices, mail should also be marked 'to be collected' (bring along your passport). Ask for the letters beginning with your initial and look through the bunch for your mail. It is not unusual for letters to 'go astray' so it's best to have mail sent to a listed address if possible.

## PUBLIC HOLIDAYS

| | |
|---|---|
| 1 January | *New Year's Day* |
| 1 May | *Labour Day* |
| 1 June | *Madaraka (self-rule) Day* |
| 10 October | *Moi Day* |
| 20 October | *Kenyatta Day* |
| 12 December | *Uhuru/Jamhuri (Independence/Republic) Day* |
| 25 December | *Christmas Day* |
| 26 December | *Boxing Day* |
| Movable Dates | *Good Friday* |
| | *Easter Monday* |
| | *Idd-ul-Fitr (day of feasting at the end of Ramadan)* |

**Islamic Festivals**. Muslim communities follow the Islamic calendar, which varies from the Western calendar by about 11 days each year. During Ramadan, the month of fasting, most stores and cafés in Islamic districts are closed during the day, particularly in the smaller towns. In 1994, Ramadan begins on 13 February. *Maulidi*, the prophet's birthday, is a colourful celebration on the coast, especially on Lamu. In 1994, *Maulidi* begins on 1st September.

## PUBLIC TRANSPORT

**Buses**. City buses operate in Nairobi and Mombasa and provide a good opportunity for seeing the city centres and suburbs at low rates. Visitors are advised to avoid peak hours, when the buses will be very **135**

crowded. The best times to use the city buses are from 9.30am to 12 noon and 2.30 to 4pm. Fares are paid on the bus.

There are no route maps on the streets or at bus stops, as these change frequently. Maps of current routes are available at the tourist office and most hotels. Inter-city buses of a reasonable standard connect Nairobi with all main centres and crowded country buses connect villages to the latter. On the faster, scheduled routes, you may need to reserve a seat a day in advance.

**Matatus**. These old, converted mini vans and small pickups are used extensively to complement the overstretched bus services between towns. Usually crammed to overflowing, *matatus* have an appalling safety record and their drivers are particularly accident-prone. To be avoided at all costs.

**Trains**. Passenger service on Kenya's single railway line from Mombasa to Kisumu is a railway enthusiast's dream. Trains are clean, cheap and supplied with good restaurant cars and well-stocked bars. Going at the leisurely pace of 55kph (35mph), the overnight trains are timed to leave the major stations of Mombasa, Nairobi and Kisumu about sunset and to arrive at these stations just after sunrise. Two consecutive nights on the train can prove tiring, however, so allow for at least one night's stopover. Thefts on all trains are common, so keep an eye on your luggage.

R

## RADIO and TV

Kenya has one English-language **radio** station that can be picked up throughout the country. The station broadcasts from 5am to midnight. You can tune in to international news at 7am, 9am, 1pm, 5pm, 7pm and 9pm. International news summaries are broadcast every hour, on the hour. On Kenya's single **TV** channel, Swahili and English programmes come on the air at 4pm and go off at about 11pm. In the Nairobi area, Kenya Television Network broadcasts CNN news and local programming round the clock.

## RELIGIOUS SERVICES

Christianity is the dominant religion of Kenya with adherents divided roughly equally among Roman Catholic, Protestant and Independent African faiths. There are also large communities of Muslims on the coast and smaller communities in the north-eastern region, where people of Somali origin live. About one-third of the rural population still adheres to a variety of traditional religions. In the urban centres, mosques and temples of various eastern faiths are much in evidence.

Nairobi is a major centre of the Independent African Church Movement. Every Sunday hundreds of groups gather on street corners, at bus stops, in parks and public halls for worship. Others march up and down the streets to the rhythm of drums in colourful clothes, carrying flags, singing and preaching. Some of the groups welcome guests, but most are suspicious of newcomers.

English services of the major Nairobi Catholic and Protestant congregations are announced in the daily newspapers on Saturdays.

S

## SIGHTSEEING and SAFARI TOURS

Numerous tour operators offer **excursions** to points of interest in the major towns and cities, as well as to game parks and other sights. Hotel chains organize their own sightseeing tours en route from one hotel to another. Ask at a tourist office or travel agent for a list of possible tours and firms, and always book your tour through a legitimate office. With advance planning, you can embark on a private **photo safari**, guided and protected by a professional armed hunter whose equipment and staff may include 4-wheel-drive cars, 5-ton lorries, trackers, camp cooks and aides. The expedition can hardly be rushed, so plan on up to a week in the Kenyan bush. This is no doubt the most exciting way of seeing the country, but the cost is prohibitive. Even a privately organized group safari is expensive and conditions are more cramped. More affordable are the numerous **special-interest safaris** and tours that cater for birdwatchers, cyclists, campers and other sports and adventure holiday activities.

**137**

## TAXIS

No taxis have meters. Whatever you do, establish the fare *before* getting into the taxi. **Kenatco taxis**, which use Mercedes Benz 200 vehicles, are recommended. They charge per kilometre and you can consult lists of approximate distances to prominent landmarks and places of interest posted in most good hotels. London-style **black cabs** are also reliable and offer more comfort and safety for slightly higher charges. **Yellow band taxis** come under the control of the municipal councils. Visitors should always check with the information bureau about the approximate charge for a journey before boarding the vehicle. **Private taxis** come under no particular control and the vehicles may not be properly insured. Charges for waiting time and extra passengers are negotiable. In addition to these, there are **long-distance Peugeot taxi services** which are shared by passengers who book their destination in advance. Prices are quite reasonable, and the ride relatively comfortable. These operate only between the major urban centres and do not go off the paved roads.

## TELEPHONES, FAXES and TELEGRAMS

**Telephone**. In theory, the Kenyan telephone service provides simple direct-dial domestic and international calls. In practice, however, this is not always so. Local and international calls are usually quite dependable, but calls upcountry, or between Nairobi and the coast can develop into frustrating, time-consuming affairs.

**Pay phone**s are painted red and can be found throughout most towns and at major post offices. To use a pay phone, simply insert the coin and dial; the coin will drop as soon as the call is answered. Local calls cost a minimum of 2Ksh, so have plenty of change. Hotel call charges are generally 50–100 percent higher than the norm.

**International calls** can be made from the main post office, where you pay for your call in advance and receive a refund if you fail to connect. Person-to-person calls are twice as expensive as station-to-station calls. There are also facilities for international direct dialling, and plastic phone cards which can be purchased at post offices and news-stands. International calls are cheaper after 10pm. Calls within East Africa are cheaper after 6pm.

**Faxes** can be sent from your hotel. There are also facilities at most main post offices, though these may be very busy.

**Telegrams** can be sent by telephone through the operator. **Telexes** are still widely used and can be sent from any post office. Alternatively, ask at your hotel reception desk for the nearest telex facilities.

**Useful Numbers**

| | |
|---|---|
| Time | **993** |
| Long-Distance Calls | **0196** |
| Dialling Assistance | **900** |

## TIME DIFFERENCES

The East African countries of Kenya, Uganda and Tanzania are on standard time, three hours ahead of GMT. It remains constant throughout the year. Sunrise and sunset times for major urban centres are published in the daily newspapers. In winter, when it is **noon** in Kenya, it is 4am in New York, 9am in London, 8pm in Sydney, 10pm in Auckland and 11am in Jo'burg.

## TIPPING

Tipping is not mandatory, but it is not forbidden in Kenya as it is in some of the African countries. On the other hand, you sometimes feel it is impossible to get anything done without offering a 'tip'. So if you appreciate a service, tip at your discretion, but keep it moderate.

Most good hotels and restaurants include a 10 percent service charge in the bill, and this is an appropriate amount to add if it isn't. At railway stations and airports 5Ksh per bag is considered usual, a bit more at hotels. It is unnecessary to tip taxi drivers, as fees should be negotiated before departure. Tour drivers, however, rely on tips to make up their wages. In general 30–50Ksh per passenger per day is adequate but can be adjusted for the quality of the service given. Guides should also be tipped accordingly.

**TOILETS** (*choo*, pronounced CHO)

Ladies and Gentlemen are almost always indicated in English, accompanied by male and female symbols. *Wanawake* (Ladies) and *Wanaume* (Gentlemen) appear in bold letters in public lavatories, and are generally warnings that the places ought to be avoided – unless in cases of extreme emergency. A 10-cent coin will open toilet doors in the public areas of hotels, but surprisingly, in the generally tourist-only areas, no charge is made.

## TOURIST INFORMATION OFFICES

Bring your queries to the local tourist office, which will recommend the best shops, car-hire firms and hotels, and advise on tours, recreation and any other subject. A wide range of guidebooks, maps and pamphlets are also available.

The Nairobi Information Bureau is centrally located opposite the Hilton Hotel, in City Hall Way, PO Box 30471; tel. 221855 (open from 8am to 5pm weekdays, 8.30am to 12.30pm Saturdays and 9am to 12.30pm Sundays).

The Mombasa Information Bureau is centrally located near the tusks on Moi Avenue, PO Box 99596; tel. 223509/220627 (open from 8am to noon and from 2 to 4.30pm weekdays, 8.30am to noon Saturdays and 8am to noon Sundays).

**Kenya Tourist Offices abroad:**

**UK**: 25 Brooks Mews, London W1Y 1LJ; tel. (071) 355 3144; fax (071) 495 8656.

**USA**: 424 Madison Avenue, New York, N.Y. 10017; tel. (212) 486 1300; fax (212) 688 0911.

9150 Wilshire Boulevard, Suite 160, Beverly Hills, California 90212; tel. (310) 274 6635; fax (310) 859 7010.

Kenya has few Tourist Offices abroad – please refer to your local Kenyan High Commission/Embassy (see p.125).

## WATER

Other than in Mombasa's hotels, Nairobi is practically the only town where the tap water is 100 percent safe for drinking. However, if you are in doubt, bottled water is always available in shops and bars. Nearly all lodges keep filtered water in jars or thermos jugs beside the bed: water from the tap is not safe, even for brushing teeth.

## WILDLIFE ORGANIZATIONS

**Mountain Club of Kenya**, PO Box 43741, Nairobi. (Members meet on Tuesday evenings at 8pm at the Mountain Club of Kenya club-house, Wilson Airport, tel: 501747 after 8.30pm.)
**East Africa Natural History Society**, PO Box 44486, Nairobi; tel. 20141.
**East Africa Wildlife Society**, Nairobi Hilton Hotel, PO Box 20110; tel. 27047.
**Wildlife Clubs of Kenya**, National Museum, PO Box 46638, Nairobi; tel. 742161.
**Museum Society of Kenya**, PO Box 40658, Nairobi; tel. 742131/2/3/4.
**Friend of Conservation**, PO Box 46613, Nairobi; tel.339537/332166.
**Wildlife Conservation International**, PO Box 20184, Nairobi; tel. 600355

## SOME USEFUL EXPRESSIONS

| | |
|---|---|
| Hello | **Jambo** |
| Good morning/evening | **Habari za asubuhi/jioni** |
| How are you? | **Habari** |
| Fine/Very well | **Nzuri/Nzuri sana** |
| Please/Thank you | **Tafadhali/Asante** |
| Goodbye/See you soon | **Kwaheri/Tutaonana** |

# Index

Where there is more than one set of page references, the one in **bold type** refers to the main entry. References in *italics* refer to an illustration.

# Berlitz – pack the world in your pocket!

## Africa
Algeria
Kenya
Morocco
South Africa
Tunisia

## Asia, Middle East
China
Egypt
Hong Kong
India
Indonesia
Japan
Jerusalem
Malaysia
Nepal
Saudi Arabia
Singapore
Sri Lanka
Taiwan
Thailand

## Australasia
Australia
New Zealand
Sydney

## Austria, Switzerland
Austrian Tyrol
Switzerland
Vienna

## British Isles
Channel Islands
Dublin*
Ireland
London
Oxford and Stratford
Scotland

## Belgium, The Netherlands
Amsterdam
Brussels

## France
Brittany
Châteaux of the Loire
Dordogne
Euro Disney Resort
France
French Riviera

Normandy
Paris
Provence*

## Germany
Berlin
Munich
Rhine Valley

## Greece, Cyprus and Turkey
Athens
Corfu
Crete
Cyprus
Greek Islands of the Aegean
Istanbul and the Aegean Coast
Peloponnese
Rhodes
Salonica and Northern Greece
Turkey

## Italy and Malta
Florence
Italian Adriatic
Italy
Malta
Milan*
Naples, Capri and the Amalfi Coast
Rome
Sicily
Venice

## Scandinavia
Copenhagen
Helsinki
Oslo and Bergen
Stockholm

## Spain
Barcelona
Canary Islands
Costa Blanca
Costa Brava
Costa del Sol
Costa Dorada and Tarragona
Ibiza and Formentera

Madrid
Mallorca and Menorca
Seville

## Portugal
Algarve
Lisbon
Madeira

## Central and Eastern Europe
Budapest
Hungary
Moscow and St Petersburg
Prague
Yugoslavia

## North America
Alaska Cruise Guide
Boston*
California
Canada
Florida
Greater Miami
Hawaii
Los Angeles*
Montreal
New Orleans
New York
San Francisco
Toronto
USA
Washington

## Caribbean, Latin America
Bahamas
Bermuda
Brazil
Cancún and Cozumel
Caribbean
French West Indies
Jamaica
Mexico
Mexico City and Acapulco
Puerto Rico
Rio de Janeiro
Southern Caribbean
Virgin Islands

* in preparation